Vegetarian Recipes
with just 3 or 4 ingredients

D0841925

WITHDRAWN

Vegetarian Recipes

with just 3 or 4 ingredients

170 simple, speedy dishes from soups and appetizers to light lunches and main courses, shown in 200 vibrant photographs

Jenny White

southwater

This edition is published by Southwater,
an imprint of Anness Publishing Ltd, Blaby Road,
Wigston, Leicestershire LE18 4SE

Email: info@anness.com

Web: www.southwaterbooks.com; www.annesspublishing.com

If you like the images in this book and would like to investigate
using them for publishing, promotions or advertising, please visit
our website www.practicalpictures.com for more information.

ETHICAL TRADING POLICY

At Anness Publishing we believe that business should be
conducted in an ethical and ecologically sustainable way, with
respect for the environment and a proper regard to the
replacement of the natural resources we employ.

As a publisher, we use a lot of wood pulp in high-quality paper
for printing, and that wood commonly comes from spruce trees.
We are therefore currently growing more than 750,000 trees in
three Scottish forest plantations: Berrymoss (130 hectares/
320 acres), West Touxhill (125 hectares/305 acres) and Deveron
Forest (75 hectares/185 acres). The forests we manage contain
more than 3.5 times the number of trees employed each year in
making paper for the books we manufacture.

Because of this ongoing ecological investment programme, you, as
our customer, can have the pleasure and reassurance of knowing
that a tree is being cultivated on your behalf to naturally replace
the materials used to make the book you are holding.

Our forestry programme is run in accordance with the UK
Woodland Assurance Scheme (UKWAS) and will be certified by
the internationally recognized Forest Stewardship Council (FSC).
The FSC is a non-government organization dedicated to
promoting responsible management of the world's forests.
Certification ensures forests are managed in an environmentally
sustainable and socially responsible way. For further information
about this scheme, go to www.annesspublishing.com/trees

© Anness Publishing Ltd 2011

All rights reserved. No part of this publication may be reproduced,
stored in a retrieval system, or transmitted in any way or by any
means, electronic, mechanical, photocopying, recording or
otherwise, without the prior written permission of the
copyright holder.

Publisher: Joanna Lorenz
Editorial Director: Helen Sudell
Project Editor: Melanie Hibbert
Copy-editor: Zoë Hughes Gough
Design: SMI and Diane Pullen
Jacket Design: Balley Design
Production Controller: Christine Ni

NOTES

Bracketed terms are intended for American readers.

For all recipes, quantities are given in both metric and imperial
measures and, where appropriate, in standard cups and spoons.
Follow one set of measures, but not a mixture, because they
are not interchangeable.

Standard spoon and cup measures are level. 1 tsp = 5ml,
1 tbsp = 15ml, 1 cup = 250ml/8fl oz.

Australian standard tablespoons are 20ml. Australian readers
should use 3 tsp in place of 1 tbsp for measuring small quantities.

American pints are 16fl oz/2 cups. American readers should use
20fl oz/2.5 cups in place of 1 pint when measuring liquids.

Electric oven temperatures in this book are for conventional ovens.
When using a fan oven, the temperature will probably need to be
reduced by about 10–20°C/20–40°F. Since ovens vary, you should
check with your manufacturer's instruction book for guidance.

The nutritional analysis given for each recipe is calculated per
portion (i.e. serving or item), unless otherwise stated. If the recipe
gives a range, such as Serves 4–6, then the nutritional analysis will
be for the smaller portion size, i.e. 6 servings. The analysis does
not include optional ingredients, such as salt added to taste.

Medium (US large) eggs are used unless otherwise stated.

Previously published as *500 Recipes: Three & Four Ingredients*

PUBLISHER'S NOTE

Although the advice and information in this book are believed to
be accurate and true at the time of going to press, neither the
authors nor the publisher can accept any legal responsibility or
liability for any errors or omissions that may have been made nor
for any inaccuracies nor for any loss, harm or injury that comes
about from following instructions or advice in this book.
Important: pregnant women, the elderly, the ill and very young
children should avoid recipes using raw or lightly cooked eggs.

Contents

Introduction

When you're tired and stressed, the last thing you feel like doing is shopping for a long list of ingredients, then going home and preparing them all before finally cooking the meal. The temptation is to grab a ready-meal or to pick up a takeaway – but when you've had a hectic day, what you really need is to sit down with a wholesome, nourishing home-made meal. This vegetarian cookery book is devoted to helping you do just that.

The good news is that vegetarian cooking doesn't need to be taxing. It's incredibly easy to make delicious dishes using just a few simple foodstuffs – the key to success lies in your choice of ingredients, and how you prepare and cook them.

The recipes in this book combine basic produce such as fruit, vegetables, herbs, spices, pasta, rice, beans and pulses, but they

also make good use of ready-made or pre-prepared products such as curry pastes and pastry. Using these convenient products saves time without compromising the taste.

When buying ingredients, always try to buy the freshest, best quality ones you can for optimum flavour and nutritional content.

It is advisable to buy fruits and vegetables when they're in season. Although most are available all year round, you can really taste the difference between those that have been ripened naturally and those that have been forced. There are so many ingredients at their peak in their own season that you don't need to buy unseasonal ones. Why buy droopy asparagus in autumn when there are plenty of mushrooms, squashes and root vegetables around, which can easily be made into any number of tasty snacks and meals?

When buying pre-prepared or ready-made ingredients such as stocks for soups or custard to make ice cream, always try to buy good-quality varieties. When an ingredient is playing an intregral part in a dish, it needs to be well-flavoured with a good texture and consistency. If you use an inferior product, it will really show in the final dish.

Whether an experienced cook or an absolute beginner, you'll find plenty of recipes in this book to suit your needs. There are dishes for every occasion: juices to quench your thirst, healthy breakfasts, soups, appetizers, light meals, and even party foods, to make when time is short. There are fabulous main courses and side dishes to cook when you have more time on your hands or if you're entertaining family and friends. There is a selection of divine vegetarian dishes to enjoy outside when the weather's sunny, and when you need a sweet treat, there are plenty of tempting desserts to choose from.

Every recipe has an ingredients list of four items or fewer, and the only other things you will need will come from the storecupboard: oil or butter to cook with, and salt and freshly ground black pepper to season the food. Some recipes use flavoured oils such as garlic-, lemon-, or herb-infused olive oil for cooking or drizzling, so it's worth keeping a few of these to hand. Occasionally, serving or garnishing suggestions are made, but these are optional extras.

No matter what the occasion, how much time you have, how many people you need to feed – you are sure to find the perfect dish within these pages.

Cantaloupe Melon with Strawberries

If strawberries are slightly
underripe, sprinkling them
with a little sugar and
grilling them will help bring
out their flavour.

Serves 4
115g/4oz/1 cup strawberries
15ml/1 tbsp icing
   (confectioners') sugar
½ cantaloupe melon

1 Preheat the grill (broiler) to high. Hull the strawberries and
cut in half. Arrange the fruit in a single layer, cut side up, on a
baking sheet or ovenproof dish and dust with the icing sugar.

2 Grill (broil) the strawberries for 4–5 minutes, or until the
sugar starts to bubble and turn golden.

3 Meanwhile, scoop out the seeds from the half melon using a
spoon. Using a sharp knife, remove the skin, then cut the flesh
into wedges and arrange on a serving plate with the grilled
(broiled) strawberries. Serve immediately.

Papaya, Lime and Ginger Salad

This refreshing, fruity
salad makes a lovely light
breakfast. Choose really
ripe, fragrant papayas for
the best flavour.

Serves 4
2 large ripe papayas
juice of 1 fresh lime
2 pieces preserved stem ginger,
   finely sliced

1 Cut the papayas in half lengthways and scoop out the seeds.
Using a sharp knife, cut the flesh into thin slices and arrange.

2 Squeeze the lime juice over the papayas and sprinkle with
the sliced stem ginger. Serve immediately.

Variation
*This summery salad is delicious made with 2 ripe peeled
stoned (pitted) mangoes in place of the papayas.*

Crunchy Oat Cereal

Serve this tasty crunchy
cereal simply with milk or,
for a real treat, with yogurt
and fresh fruit such as
raspberries or blueberries.
There are so many
variations on this theme you
could have a different
version every week.

Serves 6
200g/7oz/1¾ cups jumbo
   rolled oats
150g/5oz/1¼ cups pecan nuts,
   roughly chopped
90ml/6 tbsp maple syrup

From the storecupboard
75g/3oz/6 tbsp butter, melted

1 Preheat the oven to 160°C/325°F/Gas 3. Mix all the
ingredients together and spread on to a large baking tray.

2 Bake for 30–35 minutes, or until golden and crunchy. Leave
to cool, then break up into clumps and serve.

Cook's Tips
*• This crunchy oat cereal will keep in an airtight container for
up to two weeks. Store in a cool, dry place.
• You can use the mixture to make Cranachan as a treat,
adding Greek (US strained plain) yogurt and whatever soft fruit
is in season.*

Variations
*• You can use other types of nuts if you prefer. Try roughly
chopped almonds or hazelnuts instead of pecan nuts, or use
a mixture of all three.
• Instead of maple syrup, which has a distinctive flavour, you
could use golden (light corn) syrup or clear honey for a less
intense taste.
• Add the juice and finely grated rind of half an orange or
lemon to add a citrusy zing.
• Why not try this recipe with the addition of some dried fruit.
You could simply use raisins or sultanas (golden raisins), or chop
some ready-to-eat dried apricots or figs.*

Melon with Strawberries: Energy 46kcal/197kJ; Protein 1g; Carbohydrate 10.9g, of which sugars 10.9g; Fat 0.2g, of which saturates 0g; Cholesterol 0mg; Calcium 32mg; Fibre 1.6g; Sodium 12mg.
Papaya, Lime and Ginger: Energy 55kcal/233kJ; Protein 0.8g; Carbohydrate 13.4g, of which sugars 13.4g; Fat 0.2g, of which saturates 0g; Cholesterol 0mg; Calcium 35mg; Fibre 3.3g; Sodium 8mg.
Crunchy Oats: Energy 386kcal/1613kJ; Protein 5.8g; Carbohydrate 37.2g, of which sugars 12.6g; Fat 24.9g, of which saturates 7.5g; Cholesterol 27mg; Calcium 33mg; Fibre 3.1g; Sodium 128mg.

Muesli Smoothie

This divine drink has all the goodness of muesli, but without the lumpy texture.

Serves 2
50g/2oz/¼ cup ready-to-eat dried apricots

1 piece preserved stem ginger, plus 30ml/2 tbsp syrup from the ginger jar
40g/1½oz/scant ½ cup natural muesli (granola)
about 200ml/7fl oz/scant 1 cup semi-skimmed (low-fat) milk

1 Using a sharp knife, chop the dried apricots and preserved ginger into chunks. Put them in a blender or food processor and add the syrup from the ginger jar with the muesli and milk.

2 Process until smooth, adding more milk if necessary, to make a creamy drink. Serve in wide glasses.

Cranachan

This nutritious breakfast dish is a traditional Scottish recipe, and is delicious with a generous drizzle of heather honey. It is also wonderful served with fresh blueberries or blackberries in place of the raspberries.

Serves 4
75g/3oz crunchy oat cereal
600ml/1 pint/2½ cups Greek (US strained plain) yogurt
250g/9oz/1⅓ cups raspberries

1 Preheat the grill (broiler) to high. Spread the oat cereal on a baking sheet and place under the hot grill for 3–4 minutes, stirring regularly. Set aside to cool.

2 When the cereal has cooled completely, fold it into the Greek yogurt, then gently fold in 200g/7oz/generous 1 cup of the raspberries, being careful not to crush the berries too much.

3 Spoon the yogurt mixture into four serving glasses or dishes, top with the remaining raspberries and serve immediately.

Bananas with Yogurt and Honey

Baking bananas like this brings out their natural sweetness. If you are watching the calories, opt for low-fat Greek yogurt and leave out the nuts. Choose ripe bananas for maximum flavour.

Serves 4
2 ripe bananas, peeled
500ml/17fl oz/2¼ cups Greek (US strained plain) yogurt with honey
30ml/2 tbsp toasted hazelnuts, roughly chopped

1 Preheat the oven to 200°C/400°F/Gas 6. Wrap the bananas in foil and bake for 20 minutes. Leave the bananas to cool completely, then unwrap, place in a small bowl and mash roughly with a fork.

2 Pour the yogurt into a large bowl, add the mashed bananas and gently fold them into the yogurt. Sprinkle with the hazelnuts and serve.

Chocolate Brioche Sandwiches

This luxury sandwich is a twist on the classic pain au chocolat and beats a boring slice of toast any day. The pale green pistachio nuts work really well with the chocolate spread, adding a satisfying crunch as well as a lovely contrast in colour.

If you can't get hold of brioche, use an uncut white loaf and cut in thick slices.

Serves 4
8 thick brioche bread slices
120ml/8 tbsp chocolate spread
30ml/2 tbsp shelled pistachio nuts, finely chopped

1 Toast the brioche slices until golden on both sides. Spread four of the slices thickly with the chocolate spread and sprinkle over the chopped pistachio nuts in an even layer.

2 Place the remaining brioche slices on top of the chocolate and nuts and press down gently. Using a sharp knife, cut the sandwiches in half diagonally and serve immediately.

Muesli Smoothie: Energy 203kcal/862kJ; Protein 6.4g; Carbohydrate 40.1g, of which sugars 30.9g; Fat 3.2g, of which saturates 1.3g; Cholesterol 6mg; Calcium 163mg; Fibre 2.9g; Sodium 163mg.
Cranachan: Energy 276kcal/1152kJ; Protein 12.4g; Carbohydrate 17.2g, of which sugars 11.1g; Fat 19.7g, of which saturates 8.7g; Cholesterol 0mg; Calcium 255mg; Fibre 2.5g; Sodium 122mg.
Bananas with Yogurt: Energy 240kcal/999kJ; Protein 9.7g; Carbohydrate 14.6g, of which sugars 13.3g; Fat 17.7g, of which saturates 6.9g; Cholesterol 0mg; Calcium 201mg; Fibre 1.1g; Sodium 90mg.
Chocolate Brioche: Energy 512kcal/2149kJ; Protein 10.2g; Carbohydrate 70.5g, of which sugars 32.7g; Fat 22.9g, of which saturates 0.6g; Cholesterol 18mg; Calcium 118mg; Fibre 0.5g; Sodium 270mg.

Porridge

One of the oldest breakfast foods, porridge remains a favourite way to start the day, especially during the cold winter months. Porridge can also be a very healthy breakfast, especially if made simply with water, as oats are known to lower blood cholesterol levels and are a good source of fibre. For a treat at the weekend, brown sugar or honey can be added, and to spoil guests you could even add cream and a tot of whisky.

Serves 4

1 litre/1¾ pints/4 cups water
115g/4oz/1 cup pinhead oatmeal
splash of milk, to serve

From the storecupboard
good pinch of salt

1 Put the water, pinhead oatmeal and salt into a heavy pan and bring to the boil over a medium heat, stirring continuously with a wooden spatula. When the porridge is beginning to thicken, reduce the heat to a simmer.

2 Cook gently for about 25 minutes, stirring occasionally, until the oatmeal is cooked and the consistency smooth.

3 Serve hot with cold milk and extra salt, if required.

Cook's Tips
• *Use a whisk in place of a wooden spatula to make the porridge really smooth.*
• *Add the oatmeal in three batches to get a contrasting texture. The oats that have been cooked for the least amount of time remain slightly firm and have a nutty flavour.*

Variation
Rolled oats can be used in place of pinhead oatmeal for speed. They have slightly less flavour and lack some of the nutritional value, but cook quicker.

Eggy Bread Panettone

Panettone is a classic Italian bread made with butter and dried fruit. It can be found in most major supermarkets or Italian delicatessens. Thickly sliced stale white bread is usually used for eggy bread, but the slightly dry texture of panettone makes a great alternative. A light fruit bread could be used as a substitute. Serve with a selection of fresh summer fruits such as strawberries, raspberries and blueberries.

Serves 4

2 large (US extra large) eggs
4 large panettone slices
30ml/2 tbsp caster
    (superfine) sugar

From the storecupboard
50g/2oz/¼ cup butter or
    30ml/2 tbsp sunflower oil

1 Break the eggs into a bowl and beat with a fork, then transfer them into a shallow dish.

2 Dip the panettone slices in the beaten egg, turning them to coat evenly.

3 Heat the butter or oil in a large non-stick frying pan and add the panettone slices. (You will probably have to do this in batches, depending on the size of the pan.) Fry the panettone slices over a medium heat for 2–3 minutes on each side, until golden brown.

4 Remove the panettone slices from the pan and drain on kitchen paper. Cut the slices in half diagonally and sprinkle with the sugar. Serve immediately.

Variations
• *For a more savoury twist why not serve the Eggy Bread Panettone with some sizzling vegetarian bacon.*
• *Alternatively, you could serve it with a spoonful of strawberry jam or any other fruit compote.*
• *You could even spice it up by adding some chopped chillies to the beaten egg mixture.*

Porridge: Energy 115kcal/488kJ; Protein 3.6g; Carbohydrate 20.9g, of which sugars 0g; Fat 2.5g, of which saturates 0g; Cholesterol 0mg; Calcium 16mg; Fibre 2g; Sodium 304mg.
Eggy Bread: Energy 344kcal/1442kJ; Protein 8.4g; Carbohydrate 39.5g, of which sugars 17g; Fat 18.1g, of which saturates 7.5g; Cholesterol 151mg; Calcium 89mg; Fibre 0g; Sodium 256mg.

Apricot Turnovers

These sweet and succulent pastries are delicious served with a big cup of milky coffee for a late breakfast or mid-morning treat.

Serves 4

225g/8oz ready-made puff pastry, thawed if frozen
60ml/4 tbsp apricot conserve
30ml/2 tbsp icing (confectioners') sugar

1 Preheat the oven to 190°C/375°F/Gas 5. Roll out the pastry on a lightly floured surface to a 25cm/10in square. Using a sharp knife, cut the pastry into four 13cm/5in squares.

2 Place a tablespoon of the apricot conserve in the middle of each square of pastry.

3 Using a pastry brush, brush the edges of the pastry with a little cold water and fold each square over to form a triangle. Gently press the edges together to seal.

4 Carefully transfer the turnovers to a baking sheet and bake for 15–20 minutes, or until risen and golden. Using a metal spatula, remove the pastries to a wire rack to cool, then dust generously with icing sugar and serve.

Variations
• *Use any other fruit conserve to ring the changes, for example, black cherry or damson would be delicious and give a gorgeous colour contrast, too.*
• *For a bitter-sweet alternative use a spoonful of marmalade instead of apricot conserve. A Bramley apple purée would make a comforting option.*
• *Try a coffee filling to complement your cup of milky coffee. Just pour 45ml/3 tbsp of near-boiling water over 30ml/2 tbsp of ground coffee and infuse for 4 minutes. Strain through a fine sieve. Cream 40g/1½oz/3 tbsp butter and 115g/4oz/½ cup caster (superfine) sugar together. Beat in 1 egg yolk, 115g/4oz/ 1 cup ground almonds and 15ml/1 tbsp of the infused coffee. Place a spoonful in the middle of each square of pastry.*

Pancakes with Caramelized Pears

If you can find them, use Williams pears for this recipe because they are juicier than most other varieties. For a really indulgent breakfast, top the pancakes with a generous spoonful of crème fraîche or fromage frais.

Serves 4

8 ready-made pancakes
4 ripe pears, peeled, cored and thickly sliced
30ml/2 tbsp light muscovado (brown) sugar

From the storecupboard
50g/2oz/¼ cup butter

1 Preheat the oven to 150°C/330°F/Gas 2. Tightly wrap the pancakes in foil and place in the oven to warm through.

2 Meanwhile, heat the butter in a large frying pan and add the pears. Fry for 2–3 minutes, until the undersides are golden. Turn the pears over and sprinkle with sugar. Cook for a further 2–3 minutes, or until the sugar dissolves and the pan juices become sticky.

3 Remove the pancakes from the oven and take them out of the foil. Divide the pears among the pancakes, placing them in one quarter. Fold each pancake in half over the filling, then into quarters. Place two folded pancakes on each plate. Drizzle over any remaining juices and serve immediately.

Cook's Tip
To make your own pancakes take 150ml/¼ pint/⅔ cup milk, top up with water to make 300ml/½ pint/1¼ cups. Sift 225g/8oz/ 2 cups plain (all-purpose) flour into a large bowl. Make a well in the centre and break 2 eggs into it. With a whisk, stir in the eggs, gradually adding the milk mixture to make a smooth pouring batter. Melt 25g/1oz/2 tbsp butter and stir in with the whisk. Leave to stand for 30 minutes and stir well before using. Preheat a heavy frying pan over a medium heat. Lightly butter and add a large spoonful of batter to make a pancake about 15–20cm/6–8in across. Cook for a minute or until the underside is golden brown. Repeat.

Apricot Turnovers: Energy 279kcal/1170kJ; Protein 3.3g; Carbohydrate 39.1g, of which sugars 19g; Fat 13.8g, of which saturates 0g; Cholesterol 0mg; Calcium 38mg; Fibre 0g; Sodium 182mg.
Pancakes with Pears: Energy 544kcal/2274kJ; Protein 7.7g; Carbohydrate 64.9g, of which sugars 42.4g; Fat 29.9g, of which saturates 6.5g; Cholesterol 27mg; Calcium 155mg; Fibre 4.3g; Sodium 144mg.

Sweet Breakfast Omelette

For a hearty start to a day when you know you're going to be too rushed to have much more than an apple for lunch, try this sweet version of a simple omelette, popular throughout the Middle East, with a spoonful of home-made jam or conserve.

Serves 1
3 eggs
10ml/2 tsp caster (superfine) sugar
5ml/1 tsp plain (all-purpose) flour
bread and jam, to serve

From the storecupboard
10g/¼oz/½ tbsp unsalted butter

1 Break the eggs into a large bowl, add the sugar and flour and beat until really frothy.

2 Heat the butter in an omelette pan until it begins to bubble, then pour in the egg mixture and cook, without stirring, until it begins to set.

3 Run a wooden spatula around the edge of the omelette, then carefully turn it over and cook the second side for 1–2 minutes until golden. Serve hot or warm with thick slices of fresh bread and a bowlful of fruity jam.

Cook's Tip
Although this recipe is stated to serve one, it is substantial enough for two not-very-hungry people. Omelettes are best eaten the moment they emerge from the pan, so if you are cooking for a crowd, get each to make their own and eat in relays.

Variation
Continue the Middle Eastern theme when choosing a jam to serve with this omelette. Pick a conserve made from fruits such as fig or apricot. Alternatively, use raspberry or strawberry jam, which will be just as good.

Mushrooms on Spicy Toast

Dry-panning is a quick way of cooking mushrooms that makes the most of their flavour. The juices run when the mushrooms are heated, so they become really moist and tender.

Serves 4
8–12 large flat field (portabello) mushrooms
5ml/1 tsp curry paste
4 slices thickly sliced white bread, toasted, to serve

From the storecupboard
50g/1oz/2 tbsp butter
salt

1 Preheat the oven to 200°C/400°F/Gas 6. Peel the mushrooms, if necessary, and remove the stalks. Heat a dry frying pan until very hot.

2 Place the mushrooms in the hot frying pan, with the gills on top. Using half the butter, add a piece the size of a hazelnut to each one, then sprinkle all the mushrooms lightly with salt. Cook over a medium heat until the butter begins to bubble and the mushrooms are juicy and tender.

3 Meanwhile, mix the remaining butter with the curry powder. Spread on the bread. Bake in the oven for 10 minutes, pile the mushrooms on top and serve.

Variations
Using a flavoured butter makes these mushrooms even more special. Try one of the following:
• Herb butter: mix softened butter with chopped fresh herbs such as parsley and thyme, or marjoram and chopped chives.
• Olive butter: mix softened butter with diced green olives and spring onions (scallions).
• Tomato butter: mix softened butter with sun-dried tomato purée (paste).
• Garlic butter: mix softened butter with finely chopped garlic.
• Pepper and paprika butter: mix softened butter with 2.5ml/ ½ tsp paprika and 2.5ml/½ tsp black pepper.

Omelette: Energy 351kcal/1465kJ; Protein 19.3g; Carbohydrate 14.4g, of which sugars 10.6g; Fat 24.9g, of which saturates 9.9g; Cholesterol 592mg; Calcium 100mg; Fibre 0.2g; Sodium 271mg.
Mushrooms on Toast: Energy 230kcal/966kJ; Protein 6.1g; Carbohydrate 25.1g, of which sugars 1.6g; Fat 12.5g, of which saturates 6.7g; Cholesterol 27mg; Calcium 63mg; Fibre 1.9g; Sodium 341mg

Coddled Eggs

This method of soft-cooking eggs became very popular in the Victorian era, and special decorative porcelain pots with lids were produced by Royal Worcester from the 1890s.

Serves 2
2 large (US extra large) eggs
60ml/4 tbsp single (light) cream
chopped fresh chives, to garnish

From the storecupboard
butter, for greasing

1 Butter two small ramekin dishes or cups and break an egg into each. Top with 2 spoonfuls of cream and a knob of butter. Cover with foil.

2 Put a wide, shallow pan over medium heat. Stand the dishes in the pan. Add boiling water to half way up the dishes. Heat until the water just comes to the boil, then cover the pan with a lid and simmer gently for 1 minute.

3 Remove from the heat and leave to stand, still covered, for 10 minutes. Serve sprinkled with chives.

Boiled Egg with Toast Soldiers

Boiled egg is one of the first eating experiences many people have. Eggs and toast are nutritious, warming and comforting. Toast soldiers have a smile-a-dip quality that is just unbeatable.

Serves 1
1 egg
4 thin slices bread

From the storecupboard
a little butter, for spreading
salt

1 Place the egg in a small pan and pour in hot, not boiling, water to cover. Bring to the boil and cook for 3 minutes for a very soft egg, 4 minutes for a soft yolk and firm white, or 8 minutes for a hard egg.

2 Meanwhile, toast the bread and cut it into fingers. Serve the freshly boiled egg with toast fingers, butter and salt to sprinkle.

Potato Cakes

This is the traditional method of making potato cakes on a griddle or in a heavy frying pan. Commercial versions are available throughout Scotland as thin, pre-cooked potato cakes, which are fried to eat with a full breakfast or to enjoy with jam and butter.

Makes about 12
675g/1½lb potatoes, peeled
about 175g/6oz/1½ cups plain
* (all-purpose) flour*
jam, to serve

From the storecupboard
25g/1oz/2 tbsp unsalted
* (sweet) butter*
salt

1 Boil the potatoes in a large pan over a medium heat until tender, then drain thoroughly, replacing the pan with the drained poatoes over a low heat for a few minutes to allow any moisture to evaporate completely.

2 Mash the potatoes with plenty of salt, then mix in the butter and leave to cool.

3 Turn out on to a floured work surface and knead in about one-third of its volume in flour to make a pliable dough.

4 Roll out to about 1cm/½in thick and cut into triangles.

5 Heat a dry griddle or heavy frying pan over a low heat and cook the potato cakes on it for about 3 minutes on each side until browned. Serve hot with butter and jam.

Cook's Tip
Choose a floury variety of potato for excellent mashed potato. Maris Piper, Golden Wonder and Kerr's Pinks are all good choices, but make use of whatever varieties are available locally.

Variation
Serve with fried or scrambled eggs for a hearty start to the day.

Potato Cakes: Energy 1276kcal/5392kJ; Protein 30.4g; Carbohydrate 249.1g, of which sugars 6.7g; Fat 24.1g, of which saturates 13.4g; Cholesterol 53mg; Calcium 282mg; Fibre 14g; Sodium 203mg.
Coddled Eggs: Energy 92kcal/383kJ; Protein 6.3g; Carbohydrate 0g, of which sugars 0g; Fat 7.6g, of which saturates 2.9g; Cholesterol 196mg; Calcium 29mg; Fibre 0g; Sodium 85mg.
Boiled Eggs: Energy 409kcal/1710kJ; Protein 12.5g; Carbohydrate 40.3g, of which sugars 2.8g; Fat 23.1g, of which saturates 12.3g; Cholesterol 235mg; Calcium 154mg; Fibre 2.5g; Sodium 556mg.

Fried Egg in Butter Sauce

So simple but so tasty, fried eggs are great when you need a treat. Use the freshest eggs you can. Cook in a heavy pan and make sure the butter is hot.

Serves 1

1 egg
dash balsamic vinegar

From the storecupboard
30ml/2 tbsp butter

1 Melt 1tbsp of the butter until it begins to foam. Break the egg into it and cook for about 1 minute, until it begins to set.

2 Carefully turn the egg over. Cook for a few more seconds until the white has set. Remove and keep warm. Return the pan to the heat and add the rest of the butter. When foaming, add a dash of balsamic vinegar. Cook for a few seconds then pour over the egg.

Scrambled Eggs

Carefully cooked scrambled eggs are deliciously comforting. They cook best in a pan with a heavy base. Serve them on hot buttered toast or with grilled tomato halves.

Serves 2
4 eggs

From the storecupboard
25g/1oz butter
salt and ground black pepper

1 Break the eggs into a bowl and beat lightly with a fork until well mixed. Season with salt and pepper.

2 Put a medium heavy pan over a medium heat and add half the butter. When the butter begins to foam, add the beaten eggs. Using a wooden spoon, stir the eggs constantly as they cook and thicken, making sure you get right into the angle of the pan to prevent the eggs sticking there and overcooking.

3 When the eggs are quite thick and beginning to set, but still creamy, remove the pan from the heat and stir in the remaining butter. The eggs will finish cooking gently in the residual heat of the pan as you keep stirring. When they are set to your liking, serve immediately.

Cook's Tip
To enrich this comforting dish, stir in 30ml/2 tbsp of double cream just before the eggs finish cooking; or add 45ml/3 tbsp of crème fraîche when you take the pan off the heat.

Variation
For a tasty alternative, you can't beat scrambled eggs with cheese. For two portions, spread 2 slices of pumpernickel or wholemeal (whole-wheat) bread with butter and top with thin slices of cheese. Cut in half and set aside while you make the scrambled eggs. When cooked, spoon the eggs on to the cheese and garnish with ground black pepper.

Poached Egg

Use only the freshest eggs for this delicate method of cooking. Use poaching rings in the water if you have them for a perfect shape.

Serves 2
2–4 eggs
muffins, to serve

1 Put a frying pan over a medium heat and add 5cm/2in of boiling water. Add the poaching rings if you have them.

2 When tiny bubbles begin to gather in the water and gently rise to the surface, break the eggs, one at a time, into a cup and slide them carefully into the hot water. Leave the pan on the heat for 1 minute as the water simmers very gently (on no account allow it to boil). Then remove from the heat and leave the eggs to stand, uncovered, in the hot water for 10 minutes.

3 Use a slotted spoon to lift the eggs out of the water and drain briefly on kitchen paper. Serve the poached eggs immediately with toasted muffins.

Scrambled Eggs: Energy 240kcal/995kJ; Protein 12.6g; Carbohydrate 0.1g, of which sugars 0.1g; Fat 21.4g, of which saturates 9.6g; Cholesterol 407mg; Calcium 60mg; Fibre 0g; Sodium 216mg.
Fried Egg: Energy 297kcal/1224kJ; Protein 6.4g; Carbohydrate 0.2g, of which sugars 0.2g; Fat 30.2g, of which saturates 17.2g; Cholesterol 254mg; Calcium 34mg; Fibre 0g; Sodium 252mg.
Poached Egg: Energy 74kcal/306kJ; Protein 6.3g; Carbohydrate 0g, of which sugars 0g; Fat 5.6g, of which saturates 1.6g; Cholesterol 190mg; Calcium 29mg; Fibre 0g; Sodium 70mg.

Cinnamon Toast

This is an aromatic old-fashioned snack that is warming and comforting on a cold winter day. Cinnamon toast is perfect with a spicy hot chocolate drink or served with a few slices of fresh fruit, such as peaches, plums, nectarines or mango.

Serves 2

10ml/2 tsp ground cinnamon
30ml/2 tbsp caster (superfine)
  sugar, plus extra to serve
4 slices bread
prepared fresh fruit (optional)

From the storecupboard
75g/3oz/6 tbsp butter, softened

1 Place the softened butter in a bowl. Beat with a spoon until soft and creamy, then mix in the ground cinnamon and most of the sugar.

2 Toast the bread on both sides. Spread with the spiced butter and sprinkle with a little remaining sugar. Serve immediately, with pieces of fresh fruit, if you like.

Cook's Tips
• *Cinnamon is an effective detoxifier and cleanser, containing substances that kill bacteria and other micro-organisms.*
• *To round off this winter warmer, serve a quick cardamom hot chocolate with the cinnamon toast. Put 900ml/1½ pints/ 3¾ cups milk in a pan with two bruised cardamom pods and bring to the boil. Add 200g/7oz plain (semisweet) chocolate and whisk until melted. Using a slotted spoon, remove the cardamom pods just before serving.*

Variation
As an alternative to ground cinnamon, try using ground allspice, which is good for the digestive system. These small, dried berries of a tropical, South American tree have a sweet, warming flavour reminiscent of a blend of cloves, cinnamon and nutmeg. Although allspice is available ready-ground, it is best to buy the spice whole to retain its flavour, and grind just before use.

Welsh Rarebit

This has been a favourite snack for generations. Traditionally, the cheese is melted with butter, a little beer, mustard and seasoning, then spread on toast, but this is a quick and quirky version. It is best made with a good melting cheese, such as Cheddar, Monterey Jack or Caerphilly.

Serves 2

2 thick slices bread
10ml/2 tsp spicy or mild mustard
100g/3¾oz Cheddar
  cheese, sliced
pinch of paprika or
  cayenne pepper

From the storecupboard
butter, for spreading
ground black pepper

1 Preheat the grill (broiler) and lightly toast the bread on both sides. Spread with butter and mustard, then top with the cheese. Grill (broil) until the cheese melts and starts to brown.

2 Sprinkle a little paprika or cayenne on the cheese. Season with pepper.

Jammy Toast

The simplest snacks with minimal ingredients are often the treats that taste the best. Adding flavouring to the butter is not essential but makes a nice touch. You can use any jam on the toast, but a home-made one would taste excellent.

Serves 2

a little natural vanilla extract
grated rind of 1 lemon (optional)
4 slices bread
20ml/4 tsp jam (jelly)

From the storecupboard
75g/3oz/6 tbsp butter

1 Cream the butter with vanilla to taste until thoroughly combined. Mix in the lemon rind, if using.

2 Toast the bread on both sides. Serve piping hot or leave to cool on a rack until crisp, if preferred. Spread thickly with flavoured butter and jam, and eat immediately.

Cinnamon Toast: Energy 461kcal/1921kJ; Protein 4.7g; Carbohydrate 41.6g, of which sugars 17.3g; Fat 31.8g, of which saturates 19.6g; Cholesterol 80mg; Calcium 72mg; Fibre 0.8g; Sodium 499mg.
Welsh Rarebit: Energy 363kcal/1516kJ; Protein 17.3g; Carbohydrate 24.3g, of which sugars 1.6g; Fat 21.5g, of which saturates 13.7g; Cholesterol 59mg; Calcium 457mg; Fibre 1.1g; Sodium 687mg.
Jammy Toast: Energy 445kcal/1854kJ; Protein 4.4g; Carbohydrate 38.1g, of which sugars 13.1g; Fat 31.7g, of which saturates 19.8g; Cholesterol 80mg; Calcium 90mg; Fibre 1.7g; Sodium 475mg.

Baba Ghanoush

Adjust the amount of aubergine, garlic and lemon juice in this richly flavoured Middle Eastern aubergine dip depending on how creamy, garlicky or tart you want it to be. The dip can be served with a garnish of chopped fresh coriander leaves, olives or pickled cucumbers. Hot pepper sauce or a little ground coriander can be added too, and a sprinkling of cayennne pepper to serve.

Serves 2–4
1 large or 2 medium
  aubergines (eggplant)
2–4 garlic cloves, chopped
90–150ml/6–10 tbsp tahini
juice of 1 lemon, or to taste

1 Place the aubergine(s) directly over the flame of a gas stove or on the coals of a barbecue. Turn the aubergine(s) fairly frequently until deflated and the skin is evenly charred. Remove from the heat with tongs. Alternatively, place under a hot grill (broiler), turning frequently, until charred.

2 Put the aubergine(s) in a plastic bag and seal the top tightly, or place in a bowl and cover with crumpled kitchen paper. Leave to cool for 30–60 minutes.

3 Peel off the blackened skin from the aubergine(s), reserving the juices. Chop the aubergine flesh, either by hand for a coarse texture or in a food processor for a smooth purée. Put the aubergine in a bowl and stir in the reserved juices.

4 Add the garlic and tahini to the aubergine and stir until smooth. Stir in the lemon juice. If the mixture becomes too thick, add 15–30ml/1–2 tbsp water. Spoon into a serving bowl. Serve at room temperature.

> **Cook's Tip**
> This creamy purée can be stored in an airtight container in the refrigerator for 3–4 days.

Hummus

This classic Middle Eastern chickpea dip is flavoured with garlic and tahini (sesame seed paste). It makes a surprisingly creamy blend and is delicious served with wedges of toasted pitta bread or crudités. You can add a handful of chopped black olives too. Enjoy it with drinks or as a snack while watching television.

Serves 4–6
400g/14oz can
  chickpeas, drained
60ml/4 tbsp tahini
2–3 garlic cloves, chopped
juice of ½–1 lemon

From the storecupboard
salt and ground black pepper

1 Using a potato masher or fork, coarsely mash the chickpeas in a mixing bowl. If you like a smoother purée, process the chickpeas in a food processor or blender until a smooth paste is formed.

2 Mix the tahini into the bowl of chickpeas, then stir in the chopped garlic cloves and lemon juice. Season to taste with salt and ground black pepper, and if needed, add a little water. Serve the hummus at room temperature.

> **Variation**
> A little ground cumin can also be added, and olive oil can be stirred in to enrich the hummus, if you like.

Cannellini Bean Pâté

Serve this simple pâté with Melba toast or toasted wholegrain bread as an appetizer or snack. A dusting of paprika gives an extra kick. You can also use other types of canned beans, such as borlotti or kidney beans. Other fresh herbs will be equally good; try chervil, thyme or oregano.

Serves 4
2 x 400g/14oz cans cannellini
  beans, drained and rinsed
50g/2oz mature (sharp) Cheddar
  cheese, finely grated
30ml/2 tbsp chopped
  fresh parsley

From the storecupboard
45ml/3 tbsp olive oil
salt and ground black pepper

1 Put the cannellini beans in a food processor with the olive oil, and process to a chunky paste.

2 Transfer to a bowl and stir in the cheese, parsley and some salt and pepper. Spoon into a serving dish and sprinkle a little paprika on top, if you like.

> **Cook's Tip**
> Canned beans are usually in a sugar, salt and water solution, so always drain and rinse them thoroughly before use – otherwise the finished pâté may be rather too salty.

Baba Ghanoush: Energy 91kcal/375kJ; Protein 1g; Carbohydrate 2.2g, of which sugars 1.5g; Fat 8.8g, of which saturates 1.4g; Cholesterol 8mg; Calcium 8mg; Fibre 1.4g; Sodium 52mg.
Hummus: Energy 190kcal/798kJ; Protein 8.4g; Carbohydrate 19.3g, of which sugars 1.4g; Fat 9.4g, of which saturates 1.3g; Cholesterol 0mg; Calcium 70mg; Fibre 4.1g; Sodium 19mg.
Cannellini Bean Pâté: Energy 155kcal/650kJ; Protein 7.4g; Carbohydrate 18.4g, of which sugars 3.9g; Fat 6.3g, of which saturates 0.9g; Cholesterol 0mg; Calcium 96mg; Fibre 6.9g; Sodium 394mg.

Garlic Dip

Two whole heads of garlic may seem like a lot, but roasting transforms the flesh to a tender, sweet and mellow pulp. Serve with crunchy breadsticks and crisps. For a low-fat version of this dip, use reduced-fat mayonnaise and low-fat natural yogurt.

Serves 4

2 whole garlic heads
60ml/4 tbsp mayonnaise
75ml/5 tbsp Greek (US strained plain) yogurt
5ml/1 tsp wholegrain mustard

From the storecupboard
15ml/1 tbsp olive oil
salt and ground black pepper

1 Preheat the oven to 200°C/400°F/Gas 6. Separate the garlic cloves and place them in a small roasting pan. Don't peel them at this stage.

2 Pour the olive oil over the garlic cloves and turn them with a spoon to coat them evenly. Roast them for 20–30 minutes, or until tender and softened. Don't be tempted to speed up this process as it is necessary to bring out the sweetness in the garlic. Leave to cool for 5 minutes.

3 Trim off the root end of each roasted garlic clove. Peel the cloves and discard the skins. Place the roasted garlic on a chopping board and sprinkle with salt. Mash with a fork until puréed.

4 Combine the garlic, mayonnaise, yogurt and mustard in a small bowl.

5 Check and adjust the seasoning, then spoon the dip into a bowl. Cover and chill until ready to serve. Sprinkle over some extra black pepper before serving.

> **Cook's Tip**
> If cooking the garlic on a barbecue, leave the heads whole and cook until tender, turning occasionally. Allow to cool, separate the cloves, peel and mash.

Artichoke and Cumin Dip

This easy-to-make dip is so tasty. Grilled artichokes bottled in oil can be used instead of canned ones and have a fabulous flavour. Try chilli powder in place of the cumin and add a handful of basil leaves to the artichokes before blending.

Serves 4

2 x 400g/14oz cans artichoke hearts, drained
2 garlic cloves, peeled
2.5ml/½ tsp ground cumin

From the storecupboard
olive oil
salt and ground black pepper

1 Put the artichoke hearts in a food processor with the garlic and ground cumin, and a generous drizzle of olive oil. Process to a smooth purée and season with plenty of salt and ground black pepper to taste.

2 Spoon the purée into a serving bowl and serve with an extra drizzle of olive oil and slices of warm pitta bread.

Peperonata

This richly flavoured spicy tomato and sweet red pepper dip is delicious served with crisp Italian-style breadsticks. It also makes a tasty relish served with grilled chicken and fish dishes. It is delicious served either hot, cold or at room temperature.

Serves 4

2 large red (bell) peppers, halved, seeded and sliced
pinch dried chilli flakes
400g/14oz can pomodorino tomatoes

From the storecupboard
60ml/4 tbsp garlic-infused olive oil
salt and ground black pepper

1 Heat the oil in a large pan over a low heat and add the peppers. Cook very gently, stirring occasionally, for 3–4 minutes.

2 Add the chilli flakes, cook for 1 minute, then pour in the tomatoes and season. Cook gently for 50 minutes to 1 hour, stirring occasionally.

Garlic Dip: Energy 155kcal/640kJ; Protein 1.7g; Carbohydrate 0.8g, of which sugars 0.7g; Fat 16.4g, of which saturates 3.1g; Cholesterol 11mg; Calcium 34mg; Fibre 0.2g; Sodium 142mg.
Artichoke and Cumin Dip: Energy 42kcal/172kJ; Protein 0.6g; Carbohydrate 1.2g, of which sugars 0.9g; Fat 3.9g, of which saturates 0.5g; Cholesterol 0mg; Calcium 41mg; Fibre 1.2g; Sodium 60mg.
Peperonata: Energy 66kcal/274kJ; Protein 1.1g; Carbohydrate 6.3g, of which sugars 6.1g; Fat 4.1g, of which saturates 0.7g; Cholesterol 0mg; Calcium 10mg; Fibre 1.7g; Sodium 9mg.

Blue Cheese Dip

This dip can be mixed up in next to no time and is delicious served with pears or with fresh vegetable crudités. This is a very thick dip to which you can add a little more yogurt for a smoother consistency. Add still more yogurt to make a great dressing.

Serves 4
150g/5oz blue cheese, such as Stilton or Danish blue
150g/5oz/⅔ cup soft cheese
75ml/5 tbsp Greek (US strained plain) yogurt

From the storecupboard
salt and ground black pepper, plus extra to garnish

1 Crumble the blue cheese into a bowl. Using a wooden spoon, beat the cheese to soften it.

2 Add the soft cheese and beat well to blend the two cheeses together.

3 Gradually beat in the Greek yogurt, adding enough to give you the consistency you prefer.

4 Season with lots of black pepper and a little salt. Chill the dip until you are ready to serve it.

> **Cook's Tip**
> *Alternative blue cheeses that would work well in this dip are: the crumbly French Roquefort; the sharp yet creamy Italian Gorgonzola; the soft yet grainy Cabrales; and the spicy American Maytag Blue.*

> **Variation**
> *If you like, add a handful of finely chopped walnuts to this dip, because they go wonderfully well with the blue cheese, complementing its slightly spicy flavour. It is advisable to grind the nuts finely in a food processor to avoid the dip being too chunky in texture.*

Sesame and Lemon Dip

This delightful little dip, originating from central Anatolia, in Turkey, is often served in outdoor cafés and restaurants as a meze dish on its own – a sort of whetting of the appetite while you wait for the assortment of exciting dishes to come. In Turkey, you will see groups of old men drinking raki or refeshing tea, sharing a plate of sesame and lemon dip, tahin tarama, while they play cards or backgammon. Sweet and tangy, it is good mopped up with chunks of crusty bread or toasted pitta bread.

Serves 2
45ml/3 tbsp light sesame paste (tahin)
juice of 1 lemon
15–30ml/1–2 tbsp clear honey
5–10ml/1–2 tsp dried mint
lemon wedges, to serve

1 Beat the sesame paste and lemon juice together in a bowl.

2 Add the honey and mint and beat again until thick and creamy, then spoon into a small dish.

3 Serve at room temperature, with lemon wedges for squeezing.

> **Cook's Tip**
> *Tahin is made from sesame seeds that are ground to a fine, oily paste. This is used in several other traditional Turkish recipes, such as hummus and tahin pekmez.*

> **Variation**
> *Popular as a breakfast dish or as a sweet snack is tahin pekmez. To make it, combine 30–45ml/2–3 tbsp light sesame paste with 30ml/2 tbsp grape molasses (pekmez) to form a sweet paste, then scoop up with chunks of fresh bread. If you can't find pekmez, use date syrup from Middle Eastern and health food stores.*

Blue Cheese Dip: Energy 206kcal/855kJ; Protein 12.1g; Carbohydrate 2.6g, of which sugars 2.6g; Fat 16.5g, of which saturates 10.7g; Cholesterol 44mg; Calcium 219mg; Fibre 0g; Sodium 473mg.
Sesame and Lemon: Energy 160kcal/664kJ; Protein 4.3g; Carbohydrate 6.4g, of which sugars 6.2g; Fat 13.3g, of which saturates 1.9g; Cholesterol 0mg; Calcium 155mg; Fibre 1.8g; Sodium 6mg.

Chopped Egg and Onions

This dish is one of the oldest dishes in Jewish culinary history. It is delicious served sprinkled with chopped parsley and onion rings on crackers, piled on toast, or used as a sandwich or bagel filling. Serve chopped egg and onion as part of a buffet with a selection of dips and toppings.

Serves 4–6
8–10 eggs
6–8 spring onions (scallions) and/or 1 yellow or white onion, very finely chopped, plus extra to garnish
60–90ml/4–6 tbsp mayonnaise
mild French wholegrain mustard, to taste (optional if using mayonnaise)

1 Put the eggs in a large pan and cover with cold water. Bring the water to the boil and when it boils, reduce the heat and simmer over a low heat for 10 minutes.

2 Hold the boiled eggs under cold running water immediately (if too hot to handle, place the eggs in a strainer and hold under the running water). When cool, remove the shells from the eggs and discard. Dry the eggs and chop coarsely using a large knife with a lightly oiled blade.

3 Place the chopped eggs in a large bowl, add the onions, season generously with salt and black pepper and mix well. Add enough mayonnaise or chicken fat to bind the mixture together. Stir in the mustard, if using, and chill before serving.

> **Cook's Tip**
> The amount of mayonnaise required will depend on how much onion you use in this dish.

> **Variation**
> For a tasty alternative, spread slices of toasted ciabatta with tapenade and top with the chopped egg mixture.

Cheese with Green Olives

In Israel, mild white cheeses spiked with seasonings, such as this one flavoured with piquant green olives, are served with little crackers or toast. It is also very good for brunch – spread thickly on chunks of fresh, crusty bread or bagels.

Serves 4
175–200g/6–7oz soft white (farmer's) cheese
65g/2½oz feta cheese, preferably sheep's milk, lightly crumbled
20–30 pitted green olives, some chopped, the rest halved or quartered
3–4 large pinches of fresh thyme

1 Stir the soft white cheese in a bowl with the back of a spoon or a fork until it is soft and smooth. Add the lightly crumbled feta cheese and stir the two cheeses together until they are well combined.

2 Add the olives and the pinches of fresh thyme to the cheese mixture and mix thoroughly. Spoon into a bowl, sprinkle with thyme and serve with crackers, toast, chunks of bread or bagels.

Marinated Feta with Oregano

Feta cheese is a salty, crumbly Greek cheese that is packed in brine. The longer the cheese is left to marinate, the better the flavour will be. Serve with tomato and red onion salad and some crisp flatbreads.

Serves 4
200g/7oz Greek feta cheese
1 lemon, cut into wedges
a handful of fresh oregano sprigs

From the storecupboard
300ml/½ pint/1¼ cups extra virgin olive oil

1 Drain the feta and pat dry with kitchen paper. Cut it into cubes and arrange in a non-metallic bowl or dish with the lemon wedges and oregano sprigs.

2 Pour the olive oil over the top and cover with clear film (plastic wrap). Chill for at least 3 hours, then serve with a selection of flatbreads and salads.

Egg and Onions: Energy 197kcal/816kJ; Protein 11g; Carbohydrate 0.7g, of which sugars 0.6g; Fat 17g, of which saturates 3.7g; Cholesterol 325mg; Calcium 69mg; Fibre 0.6g; Sodium 165mg.
Cheese and Olives: Energy 242kcal/1002kJ; Protein 13.8g; Carbohydrate 0.3g, of which sugars 0.3g; Fat 19.7g, of which saturates 12g; Cholesterol 54mg; Calcium 393mg; Fibre 0.6g; Sodium 972mg.
Feta with Oregano: Energy 165kcal/684kJ; Protein 9.3g; Carbohydrate 1.3g, of which sugars 0.9g; Fat 13.7g, of which saturates 8.3g; Cholesterol 41mg; Calcium 211mg; Fibre 0.1g; Sodium 841mg.

Celery Stuffed with Gorgonzola

These stuffed celery stalks are very easy to assemble. A delicious combination of creamy cheese and crisp celery, they make a tasty addition to a picnic.

Serves 4–6
12 crisp celery sticks, with
 leaves attached
75g/3oz/½ cup Gorgonzola
75g/3oz/½ cup cream cheese
fresh chives, to garnish

1 Wash and dry the celery sticks, then trim the root ends. Leave on the leaves for an attractive finish.

2 Place the Gorgonzola in a small bowl with the cream cheese and mash together until smooth.

3 Fill the celery sticks with the cheese mixture, using a spatula to smooth the top of the filling.

4 Cover with clear film (plastic wrap) and chill in the refrigerator for at least an hour.

5 To serve, arrange the chilled sticks decoratively on a serving platter and garnish the surface of the fillings with finely chopped chives. Serve immediately.

Cook's Tip
These crunchy sticks are also ideal to serve as nibbles with drinks, but guests will find them more manageable if they are sliced into bitesize pieces rather than served whole. Use the trimmed leaves as a garnish.

Variation
If you prefer a less tangy flavour for the filling, try using Dolcelatte, which is a mild version of Gorgonzola. Exceptionally creamy, Dolcelatte will blend easily with the cream cheese and still add enough flavour to the finished dish.

Walnut and Goat's Cheese Bruschetta

The combination of toasted walnuts and melting goat's cheese is lovely in this simple appetizer, served with a pile of salad leaves. Toasting the walnuts helps to enhance their flavour. Walnut bread is readily available in most large supermarkets and makes an interesting alternative to ordinary crusty bread, although this can be used if walnut bread is unavailable.

Serves 4
50g/2oz/½ cup walnut pieces
4 thick slices walnut bread
120ml/4fl oz/½ cup
 French dressing
200g/7oz chèvre or other
 semi-soft goat's cheese

1 Preheat the grill (broiler). Lightly toast the walnut pieces, then remove and set aside. Put the walnut bread on a foil-lined grill rack and toast on one side. Turn the slices over and drizzle each with 15ml/1 tbsp of the French dressing.

2 Cut the goat's cheese into 12 slices and place three on each piece of bread. Grill (broil) for about 3 minutes, until the cheese is melting and beginning to brown.

3 Transfer the bruschetta to serving plates, sprinkle with the toasted walnuts and drizzle with the remaining French dressing. Serve the bruschetta immediately with salad leaves.

Cook's Tip
Use walnut bread slices from a slender loaf, so that the portions are not too wide. If you can buy only a large loaf, cut the slices in half to make neat, chunky pieces.

Variation
This appetizer is delicious served with a beetroot salad. Take 2 beetroots (beets), peel and grate. Place in a bowl with sliced celery (1 stick) and 2 spring onions (scallions), chopped, toss with French dressing and cumin. Season and marinate for 1 hour.

Crostini with Cheese

These irresistible cheese-topped treats will disappear in a flash!

75g/3oz thinly sliced cheese
 (Fontina or Gruyère)
strips of red (bell) pepper

Serves 6
4–6 slices day-old white or
 brown bread

From the storecupboard
ground black pepper
butter, for greasing

1 Cut the bread into small squares, triangles or circles. Preheat the oven to 190°C/375°F/Gas 5. Butter a baking sheet.

2 Top each slice of bread with cheese, cutting it to fit. Cut the pepper strips into small shapes and place on top. Grind a little black pepper over each. Transfer to the baking sheet and bake for 10 minutes, until the cheese has melted.

Bruschetta: Energy 558kcal/2321kJ; Protein 16.7g; Carbohydrate 25.6g, of which sugars 2.2g; Fat 37.2g, of which saturates 12.7g; Cholesterol 47mg; Calcium 137mg; Fibre 1.2g; Sodium 841mg.
Celery: Energy 154kcal/636kJ; Protein 4.8g; Carbohydrate 0.5g, of which sugars 0.5g; Fat 14.8g, of which saturates 9.4g; Cholesterol 33mg; Calcium 137mg; Fibre 0.7g; Sodium 327mg.
Crostini: Energy 151kcal/632kJ; Protein 8.7g; Carbohydrate 8.5g, of which sugars 0.7g; Fat 8.9g, of which saturates 5.6g; Cholesterol 26mg; Calcium 231mg; Fibre 0.7g; Sodium 387mg.

Sweet and Salty Vegetable Crisps

This delightfully simple snack is perfect to serve with pre-dinner drinks as an informal appetizer. Serve with a bowl of aioli or a creamy dip such as hummus or a blue cheese dip, and use the crisps to scoop it up. You can cook other sweet root vegetables, such as carrots, parsnips, celeriac and sweet potatoes, or even regular potatoes, in the same way. Prepare an attractive and appetizing snack by combining several different types of vegetable crisps, and then piling them together in a bowl. What could be more tempting than a pretty, colourful array of fresh, home-made vegetable crisps?

Serves 4
1 small fresh beetroot (beet)
caster (superfine) sugar

From the storecupboard
salt, for sprinkling
olive oil, for frying

1 Peel the beetroot and, using a mandolin or a vegetable peeler, cut it into very thin slices. Lay the slices on kitchen paper and sprinkle them with sugar and fine salt.

2 Heat 5cm/2in oil in a pan, until a bread cube dropped into the pan turns golden in 1 minute. Cook the slices, in batches, until they float to the surface and turn golden at the edge. Drain on kitchen paper and sprinkle with salt when cool.

> **Cook's Tip**
> *Make sure that all the vegetable slices are separate before deep-frying. Place a handful at a time in hot oil and cook until they are crisp and golden.*

> **Variation**
> *Spiced plantain chips with hot chilli sauce make a tropical and flavoursome alternative to root vegetables.*

Roasted Coconut Cashew Nuts

Serve these wok-fried hot and sweet cashew nuts in paper or cellophane cones at parties. Not only do they look enticing and taste terrific, but the cones help to keep your guests' clothes and hands clean and can simply be crumpled up and thrown away afterwards. Avoid serving these before a delicately flavoured meal.

Serves 6–8
30ml/2 tbsp clear honey
250g/9oz/2 cups cashew nuts
115g/4oz/1⅓ cups desiccated
(dry shredded) coconut
2 small fresh red chillies, seeded
and finely chopped

From the storecupboard
15ml/1 tbsp groundnut
(peanut) oil
salt and ground black pepper

1 Heat the oil in a wok or large frying pan and then stir in the honey. After a few seconds add the nuts and coconut and stir-fry until both are golden brown.

2 Add the chillies, with salt and pepper to taste. Toss until all the ingredients are well mixed. Serve warm or cooled in paper cones or on saucers.

> **Cook's Tip**
> *When preparing chillies, it is a good idea to wear rubber gloves to avoid getting capsaicin on your hands. This chemical, which is concentrated in chilli seeds and pith, is a strong irritant and will cause a burning sensation if it comes into contact with delicate skin. If you don't wear gloves, wash your hands with soap after handling chillies.*

> **Variations**
> *• Whole almonds also work well if you cannot get hold of any cashews, but for a more economical snack, simply roast whole unsalted peanuts with chillies and coconut.*
> *• Shelled pistachio and macadamia nuts can also be substituted in this recipe.*

Sweet and Salty Crisps: Energy 155kcal/639kJ; Protein 0.3g; Carbohydrate 1.4g, of which sugars 1.3g; Fat 16.5g, of which saturates 2.4g; Cholesterol 0mg; Calcium 4mg; Fibre 0.4g; Sodium 12mg.
Roasted Cashews: Energy 301kcal/1247kJ; Protein 7.2g; Carbohydrate 9.7g, of which sugars 5.5g; Fat 26.2g, of which saturates 11.1g; Cholesterol 0mg; Calcium 14mg; Fibre 3g; Sodium 95mg.

Rye and Caraway Seed Sticks

A great addition to the cheese board, these long sticks have crunchy caraway seeds inside and out.

Makes 18–20
90g/3½oz/¾ cup plain
(all-purpose) flour

75g/3oz/⅔ cup rye flour
2.5ml/½ tsp baking powder
10ml/2 tsp caraway seeds

From the storecupboard
2.5ml/½ tsp salt
90g/3½oz/7 tbsp unsalted
butter, diced

1 Preheat the oven to 180°C/350°F/Gas 4. Mix the flours, salt and baking powder together. Rub in the butter until the mixture resembles fine breadcrumbs. Stir in 5ml/1 tsp of the caraway seeds. Add 60ml/4 tbsp boiling water and mix well to form a soft dough.

2 Divide into 18 equal pieces. With the tips of your fingers, gently roll each one out to 25cm/10in long. Place sticks on a non-stick baking sheet, sprinkle over remaining caraway seeds and bake for about 20 minutes until crisp. Remove from the oven and transfer carefully to a wire rack to cool.

Salted Almonds

Served with a glass of chilled dry sherry, these delicious salted nuts make a perfect tapas dish or pre-dinner snack.

Serves 4–6
1 egg white
200g/7oz/generous 1 cup shelled
unblanched almonds

From the storecupboard
a good handful of flaked sea salt

1 Preheat the oven to 200°C/400°F/Gas 6. Whisk the egg white until it forms stiff peaks. Add the almonds and stir until thoroughly coated. Tip mixture on to a baking sheet and spread out evenly.

2 Sprinkle the salt over the almonds and bake for about 15 minutes, or until the egg white and salt are crusty. Leave to cool completely, then serve in bowls with a selection of nibbles.

Coconut Chips

Coconut chips are a tasty nibble to serve with drinks. The chips can be sliced ahead of time and frozen (without salt), on open trays. Once frozen, simply shake into plastic boxes. You can then take out as many as you wish for the party.

Serves 8
1 fresh coconut
salt

1 Preheat the oven to 160°C/325°F/Gas 3. First drain the coconut juice, either by piercing one of the coconut eyes with a sharp instrument or by breaking it carefully.

2 Lay the coconut on a board and hit the centre sharply with a hammer. The shell should break cleanly in two.

3 Having opened the coconut, use a broad-bladed knife to ease the flesh away from the hard outer shell. Taste a piece of the flesh just to make sure it is fresh. Peel away the brown skin with a potato peeler, if you like.

4 Slice the coconut flesh into wafer-thin shavings, using a food processor, mandolin or sharp knife. Sprinkle the shavings evenly all over one or two baking sheets and sprinkle with salt.

5 Bake for about 25–30 minutes or until crisp, turning them from time to time. Cool and serve. Any leftovers can be stored in airtight containers.

Cook's Tip
This is the kind of recipe where the slicing blade on a food processor comes into its own. It is worth preparing two or three coconuts at a time, and freezing, surplus chips. The chips can be cooked from frozen, but will need to be spread out well on the baking sheets, before being salted. Allow a little longer for frozen chips to cook.

Rye and Caraway Sticks: Energy 65kcal/269kJ; Protein 0.9g; Carbohydrate 6.4g, of which sugars 0.1g; Fat 4.1g, of which saturates 2.4g; Cholesterol 10mg; Calcium 12mg; Fibre 0.6g; Sodium 77mg.
Salted Almonds: Energy 269kcal/1115kJ; Protein 9.6g; Carbohydrate 3g, of which sugars 1.8g; Fat 24.4g, of which saturates 1.9g; Cholesterol 0mg; Calcium 105mg; Fibre 3.2g; Sodium 259mg.
Coconut Chips: Energy 41kcal/178kJ; Protein 0.6g; Carbohydrate 9.2g, of which sugars 9.2g; Fat 0.6g, of which saturates 0.4g; Cholesterol 0mg; Calcium 54mg; Fibre 0g; Sodium 206mg.

Plantain Snacks

Sweet and crisp, deep-fried slices of plantain are not only a great street snack, but also make excellent nibbles with drinks. The spice mixture used here – zahtar – is popular throughout North Africa and is also widely used in Turkey and Jordan. Its blend of sesame seeds, sumac and thyme is perfect with plantains, and the chilli adds a warm note.

Serves 2–4 as a snack

2 large ripe plantains
1 dried red chilli, roasted, seeded and chopped
15–30ml/1–2 tbsp zahtar

From the storecupboard
sunflower oil, for deep-frying
coarse salt

1 To peel the plantains, cut off their ends with a sharp knife and make two or three incisions in the skin from end to end, then peel off the skin. Cut the plantains into thick slices.

2 Heat the oil for deep-frying in a heavy pan to 180°C/350°F, or until a cube of bread browns in 30–45 seconds. Fry the plantain slices in batches until golden brown. Drain each batch on a double layer of kitchen paper.

3 While still warm, place them in a shallow bowl and sprinkle liberally with the dried chilli, zahtar and salt. Toss them thoroughly and eat immediately.

> **Cook's Tips**
> • *To roast the chilli, place it in a small, heavy frying pan and cook over a medium heat, stirring constantly, until the chilli darkens and gives off a peppery aroma.*
> • *If you can't get hold of the Middle Eastern spice blend, zahtar, you can make your own by combining the following ingredients in a bowl: 15ml/1 tbsp dried thyme, 15ml/1 tbsp ground sumac, 15ml/1 tbsp roasted sesame seeds, a sprinkling of coarse salt. Store the mixture in an airtight jar.*

Polenta Chips

These tasty Parmesan-flavoured batons are best served warm from the oven with a spicy, tangy dip. A bowl of Thai chilli dipping sauce or a creamy, chilli-spiked guacamole are perfect for dipping into.

Makes about 80

375g/13oz/3¼ cups instant polenta
150g/5oz/1½ cups freshly grated Parmesan cheese

From the storecupboard
10ml/2 tsp salt, plus extra
90g/3½oz/7 tbsp butter
10ml/2 tsp cracked black pepper
olive oil, for brushing

1 Put 1.5 litres/2½ pints/6¼ cups water into a large heavy pan and bring to the boil. Reduce the heat, add the salt and pour in the polenta in a steady stream, stirring constantly with a wooden spoon. Cook over a low heat for about 5 minutes, stirring, until the mixture thickens and comes away from the sides of the pan.

2 Remove the pan from the heat and add the cheese and butter. Season to taste. Stir well until the mixture is smooth. Pour on to a smooth surface, such as a marble slab or a baking sheet.

3 Using a metal spatula, spread out the polenta to a thickness of 2cm/¾in and shape into a rectangle. Leave to stand for at least 30 minutes until cold. Meanwhile, preheat the oven to 200°C/400°F/Gas 6 and lightly oil two or three baking sheets.

4 Cut the polenta slab in half, then carefully cut into even strips. Bake for 40–50 minutes, or until golden brown and crunchy, turning from time to time. Serve warm.

> **Cook's Tip**
> *The unbaked dough can be made a day ahead, then wrapped in clear film (plastic wrap) and kept in the refrigerator until ready to bake.*

Plantain Snacks: Energy 334kcal/1408kJ; Protein 1.9g; Carbohydrate 59.4g, of which sugars 14.4g; Fat 11.5g, of which saturates 1.3g; Cholesterol 0mg; Calcium 8mg; Fibre 2.9g; Sodium 4mg.
Polenta Chips: Energy 34kcal/142kJ; Protein 1.2g; Carbohydrate 3.4g, of which sugars 0g; Fat 1.7g, of which saturates 1g; Cholesterol 4mg; Calcium 23mg; Fibre 0.1g; Sodium 76mg.

Parmesan Tuiles

These lacy tuiles look very impressive and make great nibbles for a party, but they couldn't be easier to make. Believe it or not, they use only a single ingredient – Parmesan cheese.

Makes 8–10
115g/4oz Parmesan cheese

1 Preheat the oven to 200°C/400°F/Gas 6. Line two baking sheets with baking parchment. Grate the cheese using a fine grater, pulling it down slowly to make long strands.

2 Spread the grated cheese out in 7.5–9cm/3–3½in rounds on the baking parchment, forking it into shape. Do not spread the cheese too thickly; it should just cover the parchment. Bake for 5–7 minutes, or until bubbling and golden brown.

3 Leave the tuiles on the baking sheet for about 30 seconds and then carefully transfer, using a metal spatula, to a wire rack to cool completely. Alternatively, drape over a rolling pin to make a curved shape.

Cook's Tip
Parmesan cheese will keep for months if stored properly. Wrap it in foil and store in a plastic box in the least cold part of the refrigerator, such as the salad drawer or one of the compartments in the door.

Variations
• *Tuiles can be made into little cup shapes by draping over an upturned egg cup. These little cups can be filled to make tasty treats to serve with drinks. Try a little ricotta cheese flavoured with herbs.*
• *Add ground black pepper, dried herbs or finely chopped nuts to the grated cheese before baking.*

Golden Gruyère and Basil Tortillas

These simple fried tortilla wedges – a variation on the Mexican quesadillas – are great for a crowd. Fill the tortillas in advance, for a party, and cook them at the last minute. They also make a tasty late-night snack with sweet chilli sauce.

Serves 2
2 soft flour tortillas
115g/4oz Gruyère cheese, thinly sliced
a handful of fresh basil leaves

From the storecupboard
15ml/1 tbsp olive oil
salt and ground black pepper

1 Heat the oil in a frying pan over a medium heat. Add one of the tortillas, arrange the Gruyère cheese slices and basil leaves on top and season with salt and pepper.

2 Place the remaining tortilla on top to make a sandwich and flip the whole thing over with a metal spatula. Cook for a few minutes, until the underneath is golden.

3 Slide the tortilla sandwich on to a chopping board or plate and cut into wedges. Serve immediately.

Cook's Tip
Gruyère cheese traditionally comes from Switzerland. It has a slightly grainy texture and a wonderful complexity of flavours. At first the taste is fruity, but then it reveals more earthy and nutty characteristics.

Variations
• *Instead of Gruyère you could use mild Cheddar, Monterey Jack or mozzarella. If you are using mozzarella cheese, make sure that it is drained thoroughly then patted dry and cut into thin strips. Cheddar or Monterey Jack can be thinly sliced or coarsely grated.*
• *If you have a jar of pesto in the refrigerator you could spread a little over the cheese in place of the basil leaves..*

Parmesan Tuiles: Energy 52kcal/216kJ; Protein 4.5g; Carbohydrate 0g, of which sugars 0g; Fat 3.8g, of which saturates 2.4g; Cholesterol 12mg; Calcium 138mg; Fibre 0g; Sodium 125mg.
Tortillas: Energy 354kcal/1474kJ; Protein 16.4g; Carbohydrate 15g, of which sugars 0.4g; Fat 24.6g, of which saturates 13.3g; Cholesterol 56mg; Calcium 453mg; Fibre 0.6g; Sodium 486mg.

Yogurt Cheese in Olive Oil

In Greece, sheep's yogurt is hung in muslin to drain off the whey before being patted into balls of soft cheese. Here the cheese is bottled in extra virgin olive oil with dried chillies and fresh herbs to make an aromatic appetizer or party nibble. It is delicious spread on thick slices of toast as a snack or a light lunch.

Fills two 450g/1lb jars
1 litre/1¾ pints/4 cups Greek sheep's (US strained plain) yogurt
10ml/2 tsp crushed dried chillies or chilli powder
30ml/2 tbsp chopped fresh herbs, such as rosemary, and thyme or oregano

From the storecupboard
about 300ml/½ pint/1¼ cups extra virgin olive oil, preferably garlic-flavoured
salt and ground black pepper

1 Sterilize a 30cm/12in square of muslin (cheesecloth) by soaking it in boiling water for several minutes. Drain and lay it over a large plate.

2 Season the yogurt with salt and transfer on to the centre of the muslin. Bring up the sides of the muslin and tie with string.

3 Hang the bag on a kitchen cupboard handle or a suitable position where it can be suspended over a bowl to catch the whey. Leave for 2–3 days until the yogurt stops dripping.

4 Sterilize two 450g/1lb glass preserving jars by heating them in the oven at 150°C/300°F/Gas 2 for 15 minutes.

5 Mix the crushed dried chillies and herbs. Take teaspoonfuls of the cheese one at a time and roll into balls with your hands. Put the cheese balls into the sterilized jars, sprinkling each layer with the herb mixture.

6 Pour the oil over the cheese and herbs until completely covered. Store in the refrigerator for up to 3 weeks. To serve, spoon the cheese out of the jars with a little of the flavoured olive oil and spread on slices of lightly toasted bread.

Filo Cigars with Feta and Herbs

These Turkish cigar-shaped pastries are good as nibbles with drinks. The filo pastry can be folded into triangles, but cigars are the most usual shape. Here they are filled with cheese and herbs, but other popular fillings include baked aubergine and cheese or mashed pumpkin with cheese and dill.

Serves 3–4
225g/8 oz/1 cup feta cheese (mashed)
1 large (US extra large) egg
1 small bunch each of fresh flat leaf parsley, mint and dill, finely chopped
4–5 sheets of filo pastry
dill fronds, to garnish (optional)

From the storecupboard
sunflower oil, for deep-frying

1 Put the mashed feta in a bowl, beat in the egg and fold in the herbs.

2 Place the sheets of filo on a flat surface and cover with a damp dish towel to keep them moist. Working with one sheet at a time, cut the filo into strips about 10–13cm/4–5in wide, and pile them on top of each other. Keep the strips covered with another damp dish towel.

3 Lay one filo strip down in front of you and place a heaped teaspoon of the cheese filling along one of the short ends. Roll the end over the filling, quite tightly to keep it in place, then tuck in the sides to seal in the filling and continue to roll until you get to the other end.

4 As you reach the end, brush the tip with a little water to seal. Place the filled cigar, join-side down, on a plate and cover with another damp dish towel to keep it moist. Continue with the remaining sheets of filo and filling.

5 Heat enough oil for deep-frying in a wok or other deep-sided pan, and deep-fry the filo cigars in batches for 5–6 minutes until crisp and golden brown. Remove with a slotted spoon and drain on kitchen paper.

6 Serve immediately, garnished with dill fronds, if using.

Filo with Feta: Energy 311kcal/1291kJ; Protein 12.4g; Carbohydrate 11.2g; of which sugars 1.6g; Fat 24.4g; of which saturates 9.5g; Cholesterol 92mg; Calcium 278mg; Fibre 1.6g; Sodium 838mg.
Yogurt Cheese: Energy 1331kcal/5488kJ; Protein 24g; Carbohydrate 7.5g, of which sugars 7.5g; Fat 138.2g, of which saturates 33.8g; Cholesterol 0mg; Calcium 563mg; Fibre 0g; Sodium 758mg.

Cheese Straws

Everyone loves these crisp, cheesy sticks and, fortunately, they are incredibly quick and easy to make. These cheesy pastries became popular when it was customary to serve a savoury at the end of the meal, but they are perfect for serving as party snacks or with pre-dinner drinks.

Makes about 10
75g/3oz/⅔ cup plain (all-purpose) flour
40g/1½ oz mature (sharp) hard cheese, such as Cheddar, finely grated
1 egg
5ml/1 tsp ready-made mustard

From the storecupboard
40g/1½ oz/3 tbsp butter, diced
salt and ground black pepper

1 Preheat the oven to 180°C/350°F/Gas 4. Line a baking sheet with baking parchment.

2 Sift the flour and seasoning and add the butter. Rub the butter into the flour until the mixture resembles fine crumbs. Stir in the cheese.

3 Lightly beat the egg with the mustard. Add half the egg to the flour, stirring in until the mixture can be gathered into a smooth ball of dough.

4 Roll the dough out to make a square measuring about 15cm/6in. Cut into ten lengths. Place on the baking sheet and brush with the remaining egg. Put into the hot oven and cook for about 12 minutes until golden brown. Transfer to a wire rack and serve warm.

> **Variations**
> • Some or all of the cheese straws can be sprinkled with poppy, sunflower and/or sesame seeds before baking. A mixture of plain and coated straws make an attractive platter.
> • You can use other types of cheese for making the pastry. Try Parmesan, Pecorino, Mahon or, for extra colour, red Leicester.
> • Add a pinch of cayenne pepper with the cheese for warmth.

Cucumber Sandwiches

Think of Edwardian England, and afternoon tea parties with dainty cucumber sandwiches come to mind. This traditional British sandwich makes a healthy children's tea party snack, and is just as appealing to adults. Why not serve them with a glass of chilled wine.

Make 24 fingers
½ cucumber
8 slices of white bread

From the storecupboard
soft unsalted butter, for spreading
salt and ground black pepper

1 Peel the cucumber and cut it into thin slices. Sprinkle with salt, place in a colander and leave for about 20 minutes to drain. Butter the slices of bread on one side. Lay the cucumber over four slices of bread and sprinkle with pepper.

2 Top with the remaining bread. Press down lightly and trim off the crusts.

3 Cut the sandwiches into squares, fingers or diagonally into triangles. Serve immediately.

> **Cook's Tip**
> Cucumbers were first grown in English hothouses in the 16th century, just waiting for the sandwich to be invented 200 years later.

> **Variation**
> The possibilities for sophisticated sandwich fillings to be served are endless. Here are just a few to get you started: cottage cheese with cucumber; thinly sliced mozzarella and sun-dried tomato; egg mayonnaise and watercress; grated cheese with thinly sliced apple or pear; and hummus with rocket (arugula). Try varying the types of bread you use to make an appealing platter of sandwiches.

Cheese Straws: Energy 49kcal/206kJ; Protein 1.5g; Carbohydrate 3.9g, of which sugars 0.1g; Fat 3.1g, of which saturates 1.9g; Cholesterol 13mg; Calcium 32mg; Fibre 0.2g; Sodium 39mg.
Cucumber Sandwiches: Energy 174kcal/735kJ; Protein 6.8g; Carbohydrate 29.2g, of which sugars 3.3g; Fat 4.2g, of which saturates 1.1g; Cholesterol 5mg; Calcium 92mg; Fibre 1g; Sodium 307mg.

Akkras

These West African bean fritters are made in much the same way as Middle Eastern falafel. Slaves took the recipe to the Caribbean, where it remains very popular today.

Makes 20–24

225g/8oz/1¼ cups dried black-eyed beans (peas)
1 onion, chopped
1 fresh red chilli, halved, with seeds removed (optional)

From the storecupboard
vegetable oil, for deep-frying

1 Soak the black-eyed beans in plenty of cold water for 6–8 hours or overnight. Drain, then briskly rub the beans between the palms of your hands to remove the skins.

2 Return the beans to a bowl, top up with water and the skins will float to the surface. Discard the skins and soak the beans again for 2 hours.

3 Place the beans in a blender or food processor with the onion, chilli, if using, and a little water (about 150ml/¼ pint/⅔ cup). Process to make a thick paste. Pour the mixture into a large bowl and whisk for a few minutes.

4 Heat the oil in a large, heavy pan and fry spoonfuls of the mixture for 4 minutes, until golden brown. Drain on kitchen paper and then serve.

> **Variation**
> *To make classic falafels, use white beans, red onion and a large garlic clove in place of black-eyed beans (peas), white onion and fresh red chilli. Prepare as for Akkras, except do not add water, instead add 45ml/3 tbsp finely chopped parsley, 5ml/1 tsp ground coriander, 5ml/1 tsp ground cumin and 7.5ml/1½ tsp baking powder before blending. Allow to stand at room temperature for 30 minutes. Then take walnut-sized pieces of the mixture and flatten into small patties. Set aside for another 15 minutes and deep-fry until golden brown.*

Eggs Mimosa

The name 'mimosa' describes the fine yellow and white grated egg in this dish, which looks very similar to the flower of the same name. The eggs taste delicious when garnished with black pepper and basil leaves. Grated egg yolk can also be used as a garnish for a variety of other savoury dishes, such as sauces, soups and rice dishes.

Makes 20

12 eggs, hard-boiled and peeled
2 ripe avocados, halved and stoned (pitted)
1 garlic clove, crushed
basil leaves, to garnish
a few drops of Tabasco sauce (optional)

From the storecupboard
15ml/1 tbsp olive oil
salt and ground black pepper

1 Reserve two of the hard-boiled eggs and halve the remainder. Carefully remove the yolks with a teaspoon and blend them with the avocados, garlic, oil and Tabasco sauce, if using, adding ground black pepper and salt to taste. Spoon or pipe the mixture into the halved egg whites using a piping (pastry) bag with a 1cm/½in or pipe star nozzle.

2 Sift the remaining egg whites, by pressing through firmly with the back of a spoon, and sprinkle over the filled eggs. Sift the yolks in the same way and sprinkle on top. Arrange the filled egg halves on a serving platter. Grind a little black pepper over the eggs, garnish with basil leaves and serve.

> **Cook's Tip**
> *You can prepare the mimosa garnish in advance, but store the egg white and yolk separately, in small airtight containers, and keep chilled.*

> **Variation**
> *Mix 1 crushed garlic clove with 45ml/3 tbsp whipped cream and the egg yolks. Season, pipe into egg white cases and serve.*

Akkras: Energy 238kcal/1004kJ; Protein 13.7g; Carbohydrate 33.4g, of which sugars 3.7g; Fat 6.5g, of which saturates 0.9g; Cholesterol 0mg; Calcium 55mg; Fibre 5.2g; Sodium 10mg.
Eggs Mimosa: Energy 79kcal/327kJ; Protein 4.1g; Carbohydrate 0.5g, of which sugars 0.2g; Fat 6.8g, of which saturates 1.6g; Cholesterol 114mg; Calcium 22mg; Fibre 0.6g; Sodium 43mg.

Chestnut and White Bean Soup

In the north of Portugal, this soup was once prepared during Lent, the weeks leading up to Easter during which Christians were forbidden to eat meat. It is quite substantial and was a good way of supplying energy to the workers. In order to have chestnuts available throughout the year, they were dried and, before use, were soaked for about 12 hours in just the same way as dried beans. They are now readily available peeled and frozen.

Serves 4

100g/3¾oz/½ cup dried haricot (navy) beans, soaked overnight in cold water and drained
90g/3½oz/generous ½ cup peeled chestnuts, thawed if frozen
1 bay leaf
1 onion, chopped

From the storecupboard

50ml/2fl oz/¼ cup olive oil
salt

1 Put the beans, chestnuts and bay leaf in a pan, pour in 1 litre/1¾ pints/4 cups of water and bring to the boil. Lower the heat and cook for about 1½ hours, until tender.

2 Meanwhile, heat the oil in a frying pan. Add the onion and cook over a low heat, stirring occasionally, for 5 minutes, until softened and translucent. Add it to the soup.

3 Season to taste with salt, remove and discard the bay leaf and mash the beans and chestnuts with a fork. Alternatively, pulse briefly with a hand blender. Serve immediately.

Cook's Tip
If using fresh chestnuts, do not store them for more than a week. The easiest way to shell them and remove their inner skins is to make a small cut in each one and par-boil or roast in the oven at 180°C/350°F/Gas 4 for about 5 minutes. Remove the shells and rub off the skins with a dish towel. Peeled frozen chestnuts are a simpler option.

Butter Bean, Sun-dried Tomato and Pesto Soup

This soup is so quick and easy to make: the key is to use a good-quality home-made or bought fresh stock for the best result. Using plenty of pesto and sun-dried tomato purée gives it a rich, minestrone flavour. As an alternative to butter beans, haricot or cannellini beans are good substitutes.

Serves 4

900ml/1½ pints/3¾ cups vegetable stock
2 x 400g/14oz cans butter (lima) beans, drained and rinsed
60ml/4 tbsp sun-dried tomato purée (paste)
75ml/5 tbsp pesto

1 Put the stock in a pan with the butter beans and bring just to the boil. Reduce the heat and stir in the tomato purée and pesto. Cook gently for 5 minutes.

2 Transfer six ladlefuls of the soup to a blender or food processor, scooping up plenty of the beans. Process until smooth, then return the purée to the pan.

3 Heat gently, stirring frequently, for 5 minutes. Ladle into four warmed soup bowls and serve with warm crusty bread or breadsticks.

Tuscan Bean Soup

Cavolo nero is a very dark green cabbage with a nutty flavour from Tuscany and southern Italy. It is ideal for this traditional recipe. It is available in most large supermarkets, but if you can't get it, use Savoy cabbage instead. Serve with ciabatta bread.

Serves 4

2 x 400g/14oz cans chopped tomatoes with herbs
250g/9oz cavolo nero leaves
400g/14oz can cannellini beans

From the storecupboard

60ml/4 tbsp extra virgin olive oil
salt and ground black pepper

1 Pour the tomatoes into a large pan and add a can of cold water. Season with salt and pepper and bring to the boil, then reduce the heat to a simmer.

2 Roughly shred the cabbage leaves and add them to the pan. Partially cover the pan and simmer gently for about 15 minutes, or until the cabbage is tender.

3 Drain and rinse the cannellini beans, add to the pan and warm through for a few minutes. Check and adjust the seasoning, then ladle into bowls and drizzle with a little olive oil.

Cook's Tip
Try to buy canned beans that do not have added salt or sugar.

Chestnut and Bean: Energy 184kcal/773kJ; Protein 6.2g; Carbohydrate 20.5g, of which sugars 3.1g; Fat 9.2g, of which saturates 1.4g; Cholesterol 0mg; Calcium 39mg; Fibre 5.1g; Sodium 8mg.
Butter Bean: Energy 264kcal/1109kJ; Protein 14.8g; Carbohydrate 27.4g, of which sugars 3.6g; Fat 11.3g, of which saturates 2.7g; Cholesterol 6mg; Calcium 109mg; Fibre 9.5g; Sodium 932mg.
Tuscan Bean: Energy 445kcal/1863kJ; Protein 18.9g; Carbohydrate 45.8g, of which sugars 9.3g; Fat 21.8g, of which saturates 6g; Cholesterol 19mg; Calcium 391mg; Fibre 9.1g; Sodium 707mg.

Avocado Soup

This delicious soup has a fresh, delicate flavour and a wonderful colour. For added zest, add a generous squeeze of lime juice or spoon 15ml/1 tbsp salsa into the soup just before serving. Choose ripe avocados for this soup – they should feel soft when gently pressed. Keep very firm avocados at room temperature for 3–4 days until they soften. To speed ripening, place in a brown paper bag.

Serves 4
2 large ripe avocados
300ml/½ pint/1¼ cups
    sour cream
1 litre/1¾ pints/4 cups
    well-flavoured vegetable stock
small bunch of fresh
    coriander (cilantro)

From the storecupboard
ground black pepper

1 Cut the avocados in half, remove the peel and lift out the stones (pits). Chop the flesh coarsely and place it in a food processor with 45–60ml/3–4 tbsp of the sour cream. Process until smooth.

2 Heat the vegetable stock in a pan. When it is hot, but still below simmering point, stir in the rest of the cream.

3 Gradually stir the avocado mixture into the hot stock. Heat but do not let the mixture approach boiling point.

4 Chop the coriander. Ladle the soup into individual heated bowls and sprinkle each portion with chopped coriander and black pepper. Serve immediately.

> **Cook's Tip**
> *Once cut, avocados should be used immediately as they have a tendency to discolour. If you need to prepare avocados ahead of time, toss them in lemon or lime juice and store in an airtight container in the refrigerator.*

Vichyssoise

This classic, chilled summer soup of leeks and potatoes was named after Vichy, France, the home of its creator. Sharpen the flavour with lemon juice, enrich with swirls of cream and garnish with chives.

Serves 4–6
600g/1lb 5oz leeks, white parts
    only, thinly sliced

250g/9oz floury potatoes (such as King Edward or Maris Piper), peeled and cut into chunks
1.5 litres/2½ pints/6¼ cups light vegetable stock or half and half water and milk

From the storecupboard
50g/2oz/¼ cup unsalted
    (sweet) butter
salt and ground black pepper

1 Melt the unsalted butter in a heavy pan and cook the leeks, covered, for 15–20 minutes, until they are soft but not browned. Add the potato chunks and cook over a low heat, uncovered, for a few minutes.

2 Stir in the stock or water and milk, with salt and pepper to taste. Bring to the boil, then reduce the heat and partly cover the pan. Simmer for 15 minutes, or until the potatoes are soft.

3 Cool the soup then process it until smooth in a blender or food processor. Strain the soup into a bowl. Taste and adjust the seasoning and add a little iced water if the consistency of the soup seems too thick.

4 Chill the soup for at least 4 hours or until it is very cold. Taste the chilled soup for seasoning again before serving. Pour the soup into bowls and serve.

> **Variation**
> *To make a fabulous chilled leek and sorrel or watercress soup, add about 50g/2oz/1 cup shredded sorrel to the soup at the end of cooking. Finish and chill as in the main recipe, then serve the soup garnished with a little pile of finely shredded sorrel. The same quantity of watercress can also be used.*

Avocado Soup: Energy 407kcal/1676kJ; Protein 3.3g; Carbohydrate 3.4g, of which sugars 2.1g; Fat 42.2g, of which saturates 21.7g; Cholesterol 78mg; Calcium 73mg; Fibre 3.2g; Sodium 24mg.
Vichyssoise: Energy 362kcal/1494kJ; Protein 3g; Carbohydrate 11.1g, of which sugars 4g; Fat 34.2g, of which saturates 21.2g; Cholesterol 86mg; Calcium 51mg; Fibre 2.3g; Sodium 68mg.

Egg and Lemon Soup with Pasta

This light, nourishing soup, made with egg and lemon, has traditionally been a favourite throughout the Mediterranean. This Greek version contains orzo, tiny rice-shaped pasta, but you can use any small shape of pasta. Serve the soup with thin slices of lightly toasted bread and add a garnish of very thin lemon slices for a decorative appearance.

Serves 4–6
1.75 litres/3 pints/7½ cups
  vegetable stock
115g/4oz/½ cup orzo pasta
3 eggs
juice of 1 large lemon

From the storecupboard
salt and ground black pepper

1 Pour the vegetable stock into a large pan and bring to the boil. Add the orzo pasta or other small pasta shapes and cook for 5 minutes, or according to the packet instructions.

2 Beat the eggs until they are frothy, then add the lemon juice and a tablespoon of cold water. Slowly stir in a ladleful of the hot stock, then add one or two more.

3 Remove the pan from the heat, then pour in the egg mixture and stir well. Season to taste with salt and ground black pepper and serve immediately.

Cook's Tip
Do not let the soup boil once the egg and lemon juice mixture has been added, or it will curdle. Take care when using a pan that retains heat because the soup may continue to simmer after the heat has been reduced.

Variation
Substitute orzo with other small pasta, such as stellette (stars) or orecchiette (little ears). The cooking time should be the same.

Simple Cream of Onion Soup

This wonderfully soothing soup has a deep, buttery flavour that is achieved with only a few ingredients and the minimum of fuss. It makes delicious comfort food on a cold day. Use home-made stock if you have it, or buy fresh stock for the best flavour. Crisp croûtons or chopped chives complement the smooth soup when sprinkled over just before serving.

Serves 4
1kg/2¼lb yellow onions, sliced
1 litre/1¾ pints/4 cups good
  vegetable stock
150ml/¼ pint/⅔ cup double
  (heavy) cream

From the storecupboard
115g/4oz/½ cup unsalted butter
salt and ground black pepper

1 Melt 75g/3oz/6 tbsp of the unsalted butter in a large, heavy pan.

2 Set about 200g/7oz of the onions aside and add the rest to the pan. Stir to coat in the butter, then cover and cook very gently for about 30 minutes. The onions should be very soft and tender, but not browned.

3 Add the vegetable stock, 5ml/1 tsp salt and ground black pepper to taste. Bring to the boil, reduce the heat and simmer for 5 minutes, then remove from the heat.

4 Leave the soup to cool, then process it in a blender or food processor. Return the soup to the rinsed pan.

5 Meanwhile, melt the remaining butter in another pan and cook the remaining onions over a low heat, covered, until soft but not browned. Uncover and continue to cook the onions gently until they turn golden yellow.

6 Add the cream to the soup and reheat it gently until hot, but do not allow it to boil. Taste and adjust the seasoning. Add the buttery onions and stir for 1–2 minutes, then ladle the soup into bowls. Serve the soup immediately.

Egg and Lemon: Energy 107kcal/451kJ; Protein 5.7g; Carbohydrate 14.5g, of which sugars 0.8g; Fat 3.4g, of which saturates 0.8g; Cholesterol 95mg; Calcium 22mg; Fibre 0.6g; Sodium 307mg.
Onion: Energy 488kcal/2012kJ; Protein 3.8g; Carbohydrate 20.6g, of which sugars 14.8g; Fat 44.1g, of which saturates 27.4g; Cholesterol 112mg; Calcium 86mg; Fibre 3.5g; Sodium 189mg.

Pomegranate Broth

With its origins in Persia and Azerbaijan, this fresh-tasting delicate soup is perhaps the best way of eating sour pomegranates. Clear and refreshing, it is served as a palate cleanser between courses, or as a light appetizer. Sour pomegranates are available in Middle Eastern stores, but if you can only find sweet pomegranates, use them with the juice of a lemon.

Serves 4
1.2 litres/2 pints/5 cups clear
   vegetable stock
150ml/¼ pint/⅔ cup sour
   pomegranate juice
seeds of 1 sweet pomegranate
fresh mint leaves, to garnish

From the storecupboard
salt and ground black pepper

1 Pour the stock into a pan and bring to the boil. Lower the heat, stir in the pomegranate juice, and lemon juice if using sweet pomegranates, then bring the stock back to the boil.

2 Lower the heat again and stir in half the pomegranate seeds, then season and turn off the heat.

3 Ladle the hot broth into warmed bowls. Sprinkle the remaining pomegranate seeds over the top and garnish with mint leaves.

Cook's Tips
• The ruby-red grains of sweet pomegranates are eaten fresh, whereas the sour fruits are used in soups, marinades, dressings and syrups, and to make a cooling sherbet drink.
• Extracting pomegranate juice: for 150ml/¼ pint/⅔ cup juice, you will need 5–6 sour pomegranates. Cut the pomegranates in half crossways and squeeze them with a stainless steel, glass or wooden lemon squeezer to extract the juice. Do not use any metal other than stainless steel for squeezing or it will react with the astringent juice of the pomegranates, causing the juice to discolour and taste unpleasant.

Potato and Roasted Garlic Broth

Roasted garlic takes on a mellow, sweet flavour that is subtle, not overpowering, in this delicious vegetarian soup. Choose floury potatoes for this soup, such as Maris Piper, Estima, Cara or King Edward – they will give the soup a delicious velvety texture. Serve the broth piping hot with melted Cheddar or Gruyère cheese on French bread, as the perfect winter warmer.

Serves 4
2 small or 1 large whole head of
   garlic (about 20 cloves)
4 medium potatoes (about
   500g/1¼lb in total), diced
1.75 litres/3 pints/7½ cups good-
   quality hot vegetable stock
chopped flat leaf parsley,
   to garnish

1 Preheat the oven to 190°C/375°F/Gas 5. Place the unpeeled garlic bulbs or bulb in a small roasting pan and bake for 30 minutes until soft in the centre.

2 Meanwhile, par-boil the potatoes in a large pan of boiling water for 10 minutes.

3 Simmer the stock in another pan for 5 minutes. Drain the potatoes and add them to the stock.

4 Squeeze the garlic pulp into the soup, reserving a few whole cloves, and stir. Simmer for 15 minutes and serve topped with whole garlic cloves and parsley.

Cook's Tips
• Hot herb bread, with lots of chopped fresh parsley and plenty of grated lemon rind, is delicious with this broth. Mix the parsley and lemon rind with butter and spread it between slices of French bread. Reshape the slices into a loaf and wrap in foil, then heat in the oven.
• Roast shallots with the garlic, or sauté some celery to add to the simmering soup about 10 minutes before serving.

Pomegranate Broth: Energy 62kcal/260kJ; Protein 2g; Carbohydrate 3.9g, of which sugars 2.3g; Fat 4.4g, of which saturates 0.4g; Cholesterol 0mg; Calcium 14mg; Fibre 0.6g; Sodium 205mg.
Potato and Garlic Broth: Energy 75kcal/314kJ; Protein 1.6g; Carbohydrate 12.8g, of which sugars 4.8g; Fat 2.2g, of which saturates 0.4g; Cholesterol 0mg; Calcium 17mg; Fibre 1.6g; Sodium 12mg.

Winter Squash Soup with Salsa

Butternut squash makes excellent creamy soup with very few additional ingredients. Select a really good bought salsa for this soup and add a sprinkling of chopped fresh oregano or marjoram as a garnish.

Serves 4–5
1 butternut squash
2 onions, chopped
60–120ml/4–8 tbsp tomato salsa

From the storecupboard
75ml/5 tbsp garlic-flavoured
    olive oil

1 Preheat the oven to 220°C/425°F/Gas 7. Halve and seed the butternut squash, place it on a baking sheet and brush with some of the oil. Roast for 25 minutes. Reduce the temperature to 190°C/375°F/Gas 5 and cook for 20–25 minutes more, or until it is tender.

2 Heat the remaining oil in a large, heavy pan and cook the chopped onions over a low heat for about 10 minutes, or until softened.

3 Meanwhile, scoop the squash out of its skin, adding it to the pan. Pour in 1.2 litres/2 pints/5 cups water and stir in 5ml/1 tsp salt and plenty of black pepper. Bring to the boil, cover and simmer for 10 minutes.

4 Cool the soup slightly, then process in a blender to a smooth purée. Alternatively, press through a fine sieve (strainer) with the back of a spoon. Reheat without boiling, then ladle it into warmed bowls. Top each serving with a spoonful of salsa and serve.

Cook's Tip
To make your own salsa: roast 4 large ripe tomatoes, halved and seeded, 1 red (bell) pepper, seeded, 1 large red chilli, halved and seeded, in a fairly hot oven for 25 minutes. Allow to cool, then skin the pepper and chilli. Blend briefly in a food processor with tomatoes and 30ml/2 tbsp extra virgin olive oil. Stir in 15ml/1 tbsp balsamic vinegar and a pinch of caster (superfine) sugar. Season, then serve.

Pea Soup with Garlic

A great standby lunch dish or appetizer, if you keep peas in the freezer, you can rustle up this delicious soup in minutes. It has a sweet taste, smooth texture and vibrant colour and is great served with crusty bread and garnished with mint.

Serves 4
1 garlic clove, crushed
900g/2lb/8 cups frozen peas
1.2 litres/2 pints/5 cups
    vegetable stock

From the storecupboard
25g/1oz/2 tbsp butter
salt and ground black pepper

1 Heat the butter in a large heavy pan until just foaming and add the garlic. Fry gently for 2–3 minutes, until softened, then add the frozen peas. Cook for 1–2 minutes more, then pour in the stock.

2 Bring the soup to the boil, then reduce the heat to a simmer. Cover the pan and cook for 5–6 minutes, until the peas are tender. Leave to cool slightly, then transfer the mixture to a food processor and process until smooth (you may have to do this in two batches).

3 Return the soup to the rinsed pan and heat through gently. Season with salt and pepper.

Variations
• *Iced pea soup is food for hot summer days. Use frozen petits pois (baby peas) for a sweet flavour and add the grated rind and juice of 1 lime to the cold soup.*
• *Crisp cubes of pan-fried halloumi cheese are delicious in this plain pea soup. Have the pan hot, the soup ready in warm bowls and then cook cubes of cheese quickly until brown outside and soft inside. Float in the soup and serve.*
• *Sprinkle with a little finely shredded fresh sage and a handful of croutons, to garnish.*
• *Serve the hot soup with shavings of Parmesan cheese and plenty of ground black pepper.*

Winter Squash Soup: Energy 172kcal/712kJ; Protein 2.7g; Carbohydrate 12.6g, of which sugars 9.3g; Fat 12.6g, of which saturates 2g; Cholesterol 0mg; Calcium 86mg; Fibre 3.6g; Sodium 4mg.
Pea with Garlic: Energy 233kcal/965kJ; Protein 15.6g; Carbohydrate 25.5g, of which sugars 5.2g; Fat 8.5g, of which saturates 3.9g; Cholesterol 13mg; Calcium 49mg; Fibre 10.6g; Sodium 40mg.

Curried Cauliflower Soup

This spicy, velvety soup is perfect for lunch on a cold winter's day served with a large chunk of warm crusty bread and garnished with a sprinkling of fragrant fresh coriander (cilantro).

Serves 4

750ml/1¼ pints/3 cups milk
1 large cauliflower
15ml/1 tbsp garam masala

From the storecupboard
salt and ground black pepper

1 Pour the milk into a large pan and place over a medium heat. Cut the cauliflower into florets and add to the milk with the garam masala. Season with salt and pepper.

2 Bring the milk to the boil, then reduce the heat, partially cover the pan with a lid and simmer for about 20 minutes, or until the cauliflower is tender.

3 Let the mixture cool for a few minutes, then transfer to a food processor and process until smooth (you may have to do this in two batches). Return the purée to the pan and heat through gently, checking and adjusting the seasoning. Serve immediately.

Cook's Tip
You can use all parts of the cauliflower to bring an excellent flavour to this soup. Just trim off any wilted or damaged leaves and the very tough stalk. Then cut off the florets, cut the stalks into a small dice and thinly slice the leaves.

Variations
• Cauliflower lends itself wonderfully to mildy curried recipes, but you can also make broccoli soup in the same way, using the same weight of broccoli in place of the cauliflower.
• Parsnips are also complemented by curry flavours. Try this recipe with 4 large parsnips, peeled and chopped into large chunks and cooked until tender.

Stilton and Watercress Soup

A good creamy Stilton and plenty of peppery watercress bring maximum flavour to this rich, smooth soup, which is superlative in small portions. Rocket can be used as an alternative to watercress – both leaves are an excellent source of iron. When choosing any salad leaves, look for crisp, fresh leaves and reject any wilted or discoloured greens.

Serves 4–6

600ml/1 pint/2½ cups
  vegetable stock
225g/8oz watercress
150g/5oz Stilton or other
  blue cheese
150ml/¼ pint/⅔ cup single
  (light) cream

1 Pour the stock into a pan and bring almost to the boil. Remove and discard any very large stalks from the watercress. Add the watercress to the pan and simmer gently for 2–3 minutes, until tender.

2 Crumble the cheese into the pan and simmer for 1 minute more, until the cheese has started to melt. Process the soup in a blender or food processor, in batches if necessary, until very smooth. Return the soup to the pan.

3 Stir in the cream and check the seasoning. The soup will probably not need any extra salt, as the blue cheese is already quite salty. Heat the soup gently, without boiling, then ladle it into warm bowls.

Cook's Tip
To make your vegetable stock put 900g/2lb chopped vegetables, including onions, leeks, tomatoes, carrots, parsnips and cabbage, in a large pan. Pour in 1.5 litres/2½ pints/6¼ cups water. Bring to the boil and simmer for 30 minutes. Strain into a container and discard the cooked vegetables. The stock can then be frozen for up to 3 months.

Stilton Soup: Energy 159kcal/659kJ; Protein 7.9g; Carbohydrate 0.7g, of which sugars 0.7g; Fat 13.7g, of which saturates 8.9g; Cholesterol 38mg; Calcium 168mg; Fibre 0.6g; Sodium 223mg.
Curried Cauliflower: Energy 151kcal/636kJ; Protein 12.9g; Carbohydrate 14.7g, of which sugars 13.2g; Fat 5g, of which saturates 2.4g; Cholesterol 11mg; Calcium 276mg; Fibre 3.7g; Sodium 107mg.

Miso Broth with Mushrooms

This broth is so quick and simple to prepare, yet extremely delicious and nutritious too. Shiitake mushrooms give this soup superb flavour.

Serves 4
45ml/3 tbsp light miso paste
3 fresh shiitake mushrooms, sliced
115g/4oz tofu, diced
1 spring onion (scallion), green
part only, sliced

1 Mix 1.2 litres/2 pints/5 cups boiling water and miso in a pan. Add the mushrooms and simmer for 5 minutes. Divide the tofu among four warmed soup bowls, ladle in the soup, sprinkle with sliced spring onions and serve.

Wheat Noodles in Soya Bean Soup

Strands of thin wheat noodles taste great in a mild and deliciously nutty chilled soup. This is a perfect choice of satisfying soup for a warm summer's day. The iced broth is topped with succulent strips of cucumber and wedges of tomato, providing refreshing flavours to complement the tender noodles.

Serves 4
185g/6½oz/1 cup soya beans
30ml/2 tbsp sesame seeds
300g/11oz thin wheat noodles

From the storecupboard
salt

For the garnish (optional)
1 cucumber, cut into thin strips
1 tomato, cut into wedges

1 Soak the soya beans overnight. Rinse in cold water and then roll them between your palms to remove the skins.

2 Gently toast the sesame seeds in a dry pan until they are lightly browned. Place the peeled soya beans and the sesame seeds in a food processor or blender. Add 1 litre/1¾ pints/ 4 cups water and process until the beans and seeds are finely ground.

3 Strain the bean mixture through muslin (cheesecloth), collecting the liquid in a jug (pitcher) – this is soya and sesame milk. Chill the soya and sesame milk in the refrigerator.

4 Bring a pan of water to the boil and cook the noodles, then drain them and rinse in cold water.

5 Place a portion of noodles in each soup bowl, and pour over the chilled milk. Garnish with strips of cucumber and tomato wedges, then season with salt and serve.

Variation
For a quick and easy version, use 250ml/8fl oz/1 cup unsweetened soya milk rather than soaking and puréeing the soya beans. Simply add the ground sesame seeds to the soya milk and chill to make the soup.

Star-gazer Vegetable Soup

If you have the time, it is worth making your own stock for this recipe.

Serves 4
1 yellow (bell) pepper and
2 large courgettes (zucchini)

2 large carrots
900ml/1½ pints/3¾ cups well-
flavoured vegetable stock
50g/2oz rice vermicelli

From the storecupboard
salt and ground black pepper

1 Cut the pepper into quarters, removing the seeds and core. Chop the courgettes and carrots lengthways into 5mm/¼in slices.

2 Using tiny pastry cutters, stamp out shapes from the vegetables or use a very sharp knife to cut the sliced vegetables into stars and other decorative shapes.

3 Place the vegetables and stock in a pan and simmer for 10 minutes, until the vegetables are tender. Season to taste with salt and pepper.

4 Meanwhile, place the vermicelli in a bowl, cover with boiling water and set aside for 4 minutes. Drain, then divide among four warmed soup bowls. Ladle over the soup and serve with fresh bread.

Wheat Noodles: Energy 268kcal/1121kJ; Protein 20.1g; Carbohydrate 17.9g, of which sugars 3.4g; Fat 13.3g, of which saturates 1.7g; Cholesterol 0mg; Calcium 174mg; Fibre 8.7g; Sodium 6mg.
Miso Broth: Energy 25kcal/103kJ; Protein 2.4g; Carbohydrate 2.6g, of which sugars 2.4g; Fat 0.6g, of which saturates 0.1g; Cholesterol 0mg; Calcium 107mg; Fibre 1.6g; Sodium 882mg.
Star-gazer Soup: Energy 96kcal/399kJ; Protein 3.4g; Carbohydrate 19.1g, of which sugars 8.9g; Fat 0.8g, of which saturates 0.2g; Cholesterol 0mg; Calcium 58mg; Fibre 3.1g; Sodium 20mg.

Onion Cake

Serve this simple but delicious dish alone or with a salad accompaniment as an appetizer. The cooking time will depend on the potatoes that you use and how thinly they are sliced: use a food processor or mandolin (if you have one) to make paper-thin slices. The mound of potatoes will cook down to make a thick buttery cake.

Serves 6
900g/2lb new potatoes, peeled and thinly sliced
2 medium onions, very finely chopped

From the storecupboard
salt and ground black pepper
about 115g/4oz/½ cup butter

1 Preheat the oven to 190°C/375°F/Gas 5. Grease a 20cm/8in round cake tin (pan) with butter and line the base with a circle of baking parchment.

2 Arrange some of the potato slices evenly in the bottom of the tin and then sprinkle some of the onions over them. Season with salt and pepper. Reserve 25g/1oz/2 tbsp of the butter and dot the mixture with tiny pieces of the remaining butter.

3 Repeat these layers, using up all the ingredients and finishing with a layer of potatoes. Melt the reserved butter and brush it over the top.

4 Cover the potatoes with foil, put in the hot oven and cook for 1–1½ hours, until tender and golden. Remove from the oven and leave to stand, still covered, for 10–15 minutes.

5 Carefully turn out on to a warmed plate and serve.

> **Cook's Tip**
> *If using old potatoes, cook and serve them in an earthenware or ovenproof glass dish. Remove the cover from the dish for the final 10–15 minutes to lightly brown the top.*

Mushroom Caviar

The name mushroom caviar refers to the dark colour and texture of this dish of chopped mushrooms. Serve the mixture in individual serving dishes with toasted rye bread, or sourdough, rubbed with cut garlic cloves, to complement the rich earthy flavour of the mushrooms. Chopped hard-boiled egg, spring onion and parsley, the traditional garnishes for caviar, can be served as a garnish.

Serves 4
450g/1lb mushrooms, coarsely chopped
5–10 shallots, chopped
4 garlic cloves, chopped

From the storecupboard
45ml/3 tbsp olive or vegetable oil

1 Heat the oil in a large pan, add the mushrooms, shallots and garlic, and cook, stirring occasionally, until browned. Season with salt, then continue cooking until the mushrooms give up their liquor.

2 Continue cooking, stirring frequently, until the liquor has evaporated and the mushrooms are brown and dry.

3 Put the mixture in a food processor or blender and process briefly until a chunky paste is formed. Spoon the mushroom caviar into dishes and serve.

> **Cook's Tip**
> *If garnishing with eggs, prevent black rings from forming around the egg yolks by cracking the shells all over as soon as the eggs are cooked, and cool quickly in cold water.*

> **Variation**
> *For a rich wild mushroom caviar, soak 10–15g/¼–½oz dried porcini in about 120ml/4fl oz/½ cup water for about 30 minutes. Add the porcini and their soaking liquid to the browned mushrooms in step 2. Continue as in the recipe. Serve with wedges of lemon, for their tangy juice.*

Onion Cake: Energy 272kcal/1133kJ; Protein 3.5g; Carbohydrate 29.5g, of which sugars 5.8g; Fat 16.3g, of which saturates 10.1g; Cholesterol 41mg; Calcium 29mg; Fibre 2.4g; Sodium 135mg.
Mushroom Caviar: Energy 68kcal/283kJ; Protein 3.3g; Carbohydrate 6.4g, of which sugars 3.8g; Fat 3.5g, of which saturates 0.5g; Cholesterol 0mg; Calcium 24mg; Fibre 2.4g; Sodium 8mg.

Baked Eggs with Creamy Leeks

This simple but elegant dish is perfect for last-minute entertaining or quick dining. Garnish the baked eggs with crisp, fried fresh sage leaves and serve with warm, crusty bread. Small to medium leeks (less than 2.5cm/1in in diameter) are best for this dish as they are so tender and only require a short cooking time.

Serves 4

225g/8oz small leeks, thinly sliced
75–90ml/5–6 tbsp
  whipping cream
4 small–medium
  (US medium–large) eggs

From the storecupboard
15g/½oz/1 tbsp butter, plus extra
  for greasing
salt and ground black pepper

1 Preheat the oven to 190°C/375°F/Gas 5. Generously butter the base and sides of four ramekins.

2 Melt the butter in a frying pan and cook the leeks over a medium heat, stirring frequently, for 3–5 minutes, until softened and translucent, but not browned.

3 Add 45ml/3 tbsp of the cream and cook over a low heat for 5 minutes, until the leeks are very soft and the cream has thickened a little. Season to taste.

4 Place the ramekins in a small roasting pan and divide the leeks among them. Break an egg into each dish, spoon over the remaining cream and season. Pour boiling water into the roasting pan to come about halfway up the sides of the ramekins. Transfer the pan to the oven and bake in the preheated oven for about 10 minutes, until just set. Serve piping hot.

> **Variation**
> For a stunning alternative, simply break large (US extra large) eggs into ramekin dishes, pour double (heavy) cream over, season and sprinkle generously with Parmesan cheese. Bake for 10 minutes at 160°C/325°F/Gas 3.

Pea and Mint Omelette

Serve this deliciously light omelette with crusty bread and a green salad for a fresh, tasty lunch. If you're making the omelette for a summer lunch when peas are in season, use freshly shelled peas instead of frozen ones.

Serves 2

50g/2oz/½ cup frozen peas
4 eggs
30ml/2 tbsp chopped fresh mint

From the storecupboard
knob (pat) of butter
salt and ground black pepper

1 Cook the peas in a large pan of salted boiling water for 3–4 minutes until tender. Drain well and set aside. Break the eggs into a large bowl and beat with a fork. Season well with salt and pepper, then stir in the peas and chopped mint.

2 Heat the butter in a medium frying pan until foamy. Pour in the egg mixture and cook over a medium heat for 3–4 minutes, drawing in the cooked egg from the edges from time to time, until the mixture is nearly set.

3 Finish off cooking the omelette under a hot grill (broiler) until set and golden. Carefully fold the omelette over, cut it in half and serve immediately.

> **Cook's Tip**
> Although special omelette pans are available, any heavy, medium non-stick frying pan will be sufficient.

> **Variations**
> • This omelette can also be served cold and cut into wedges or fingers as an appetizer or to serve with drinks at a party.
> • You could also try using lightly sautéed spinach or courgette (zucchini) instead of peas.
> • Sun-dried tomatoes and onion with a pinch of thyme make a flavoursome alternative.

Baked Eggs: Energy 149kcal/614kJ; Protein 4.4g; Carbohydrate 2.2g, of which sugars 1.8g; Fat 13.7g, of which saturates 7.5g; Cholesterol 123mg; Calcium 39mg; Fibre 1.3g; Sodium 64mg.
Omelette: Energy 205kcal/851kJ; Protein 14.3g; Carbohydrate 2.9g, of which sugars 0.6g; Fat 15.6g, of which saturates 5.8g; Cholesterol 391mg; Calcium 63mg; Fibre 1.2g; Sodium 171mg.

Fried Mozzarella Sandwich

This is reassuring snacking Italian style, with glorious melting mozzarella in crisp fried egg-soaked bread. The result is a delicious savoury sandwich guaranteed to lift the spirits.

Makes 2
115g/4oz/1 cup mozzarella
   cheese, thickly sliced
4 thick slices white bread
1 egg
30ml/2 tbsp milk

From the storecupboard
vegetable oil, for frying
salt and ground black pepper

1 Place the cheese on two slices of bread and season to taste. Top with the remaining bread to make two cheese sandwiches.

2 Beat the egg with the milk. Season with salt and pepper to taste and pour into a shallow dish.

3 Carefully dip the sandwiches into the egg and milk mixture until thoroughly coated. Leave to soak while heating the oil in a large, heavy frying pan.

4 Fry the sandwiches, in batches if necessary, until golden brown and crisp on both sides. Remove from the frying pan and drain well on kitchen paper.

Variation
Use any favourite cheese instead of mozzarella. You could also try adding some chopped spring onions (scallions) before sandwiching the bread together.

Toasted Sourdough with Goat's Cheese

The combination of sharp cheese with sweet and spicy chilli jam is truly delicious. Choose a good-quality, firm goat's cheese for this recipe because it needs to keep its shape during cooking. Serve with fresh rocket (arugula) leaves.

Serves 2
2 thick sourdough bread slices
30ml/2 tbsp chilli jam
2 firm goat's cheese slices, about
   90g/3½oz each

From the storecupboard
30ml/2 tbsp garlic-infused olive oil
ground black pepper

1 Preheat the grill (broiler) to high. Brush the sourdough bread on both sides with the oil, and grill (broil) one side until golden. Spread the untoasted side of each slice with the chilli jam and top with the goat's cheese.

2 Return the bread to the grill and cook for 3–4 minutes, or until the cheese is beginning to melt and turn golden and bubbling. Season with ground black pepper and serve while hot.

Griddled Tomatoes on Soda Bread

Nothing could be easier than this simple dish, transformed into something really special by adding a drizzle of olive oil, balsamic vinegar and shavings of Parmesan cheese.

Serves 4
6 tomatoes, thickly sliced
4 thick slices soda bread
balsamic vinegar, for drizzling
shavings of Parmesan cheese,
   to serve

From the storecupboard
olive oil, for brushing and drizzling
salt and ground black pepper

1 Brush a griddle pan with olive oil and heat. Add the tomato slices and cook for 4–6 minutes, turning once, until softened and slightly blackened. Alternatively, heat a grill (broiler) to high and line the rack with foil. Grill (broil) the tomato slices for 4–6 minutes, turning once, until softened.

2 While the tomatoes are cooking, lightly toast the soda bread. Place the tomatoes on top of the toast and drizzle each portion with a little olive oil and vinegar. Season to taste and serve immediately with thin shavings of Parmesan.

Cook's Tip
Using a griddle pan reduces the amount of oil required for cooking the tomatoes and gives them a smoky barbecued flavour. The ridges on the pan brand the tomatoes with a stripy pattern, which looks very appealing. To make a cross-hatched pattern, turn the tomato slices 180 degrees halfway through the cooking time.

Variation
You could enhance this simple, yet flavoursome, dish further by using an infused oil, such as lemon oil, chilli oil, garlic oil or herb-infused oil. These are all available in supermarkets or can be made easily at home.

Fried Mozzarella: Energy 429kcal/1789kJ; Protein 18.9g; Carbohydrate 30.5g, of which sugars 2.7g; Fat 26.6g, of which saturates 10.4g; Cholesterol 129mg; Calcium 331mg; Fibre 1.9g; Sodium 539mg.
Toasted Sourdough: Energy 533kcal/2225kJ; Protein 23.4g; Carbohydrate 33g, of which sugars 9.5g; Fat 35.2g, of which saturates 17.7g; Cholesterol 84mg; Calcium 178mg; Fibre 1g; Sodium 826mg.
Tomatoes on Soda Bread: Energy 178kcal/751kJ; Protein 4.2g; Carbohydrate 26.3g, of which sugars 6.9g; Fat 7g, of which saturates 1g; Cholesterol 0mg; Calcium 66mg; Fibre 2.7g; Sodium 175mg.

Baked Sweet Potatoes with Leeks and Gorgonzola

The smoky sweetness of the potatoes is perfectly balanced by the piquancy of the Gorgonzola cheese in this warming lunch dish. Not only does it taste wonderful, but it looks stunning too, if you use the vibrant orange-fleshed sweet potatoes.

Serves 4
4 large sweet potatoes, scrubbed
2 large leeks, washed and sliced
115g/4oz/1 cup Gorgonzola
   cheese, sliced

From the storecupboard
30ml/2 tbsp olive oil
salt and ground black pepper

1 Preheat the oven to 190°C/375°F/Gas 5. Dry the sweet potatoes with kitchen paper and rub them all over with 15ml/1 tbsp of the oil. Place them on a baking sheet and sprinkle with salt. Bake for 1 hour, or until tender.

2 Meanwhile, heat the remaining oil in a frying pan and add the sliced leeks. Cook for 3–4 minutes, or until softened and just beginning to turn golden.

3 Cut the potatoes in half lengthways and place them cut side up on the baking sheet. Top with the cooked leeks and season.

4 Lay the cheese slices on top and grill (broil) under a hot grill for 2–3 minutes, until the cheese is bubbling. Serve immediately.

Cook's Tip
Select evenly sized sweet potatoes with unblemished skins and wash them thoroughly before using. If the potatoes are cooked before you need them, wrap them in a warmed cloth.

Variation
Instead of the Italian Gorgonzola cheese you could use other blue cheeses, such as, Danish Blue, Roquefort or Stilton.

Roasted Pepper and Hummus Wrap

Wraps make a tasty change from sandwiches and have the bonus that they can be made a few hours in advance without going soggy in the way that bread sandwiches often can. You can introduce all kinds of variation to this basic combination. Try using roasted aubergine in place of the red peppers, or guacamole in place of the hummus.

Serves 2
1 large red (bell) pepper, halved
   and seeded
60ml/4 tbsp hummus
2 soft flour tortillas

From the storecupboard
15ml/1 tbsp olive oil
salt and ground black pepper

1 Preheat the grill (broiler) to high. Brush the pepper halves with the oil and place cut side down on a baking sheet. Grill (broil) for 5 minutes, until charred. Put the pepper halves in a sealed plastic bag and leave to cool.

2 When cooled, remove the peppers from the bag and carefully peel away the charred skin and discard. Thinly slice the flesh using a sharp knife.

3 Spread the hummus over the tortillas in a thin, even layer and top with the roasted pepper slices. Season with salt and plenty of ground black pepper, then roll them up and cut in half to serve.

Marinated Courgette and Flageolet Bean Salad

Serve this healthy salad as a light lunch or as an accompaniment to a main course. It has a wonderful bright green colour and is perfect for summer dining. To give extra flavour to the salad add chopped fresh herbs before chilling. Basil and mint both have fresh, distinctive flavours that work well with the courgettes and beans.

Serves 4
2 courgettes (zucchini), halved
   lengthways and sliced
400g/14oz can flageolet or
   cannellini beans, drained
   and rinsed
grated rind and juice of
   1 unwaxed lemon

From the storecupboard
45ml/3 tbsp garlic-infused olive oil
salt and ground black pepper

1 Cook the courgettes in boiling salted water for 2–3 minutes, or until just tender. Drain well and refresh under cold running water.

2 Transfer the drained courgettes to a bowl with the beans and stir in the oil, lemon rind and juice and some salt and pepper. Chill for 30 minutes before serving.

Sweet Potatoes: Energy 338kcal/1425kJ; Protein 9.5g; Carbohydrate 44.8g, of which sugars 13.1g; Fat 14.8g, of which saturates 6.6g; Cholesterol 22mg; Calcium 206mg; Fibre 6.5g; Sodium 432mg.
Pepper Wrap: Energy 265kcal/1112kJ; Protein 6.8g; Carbohydrate 39g, of which sugars 6.5g; Fat 10.1g, of which saturates 0.9g; Cholesterol 0mg; Calcium 75mg; Fibre 3.3g; Sodium 345mg.
Courgette and Bean Salad: Energy 106kcal/444kJ; Protein 5.5g; Carbohydrate 11.9g, of which sugars 3.5g; Fat 4.4g, of which saturates 0.7g; Cholesterol 0mg; Calcium 62mg; Fibre 4.4g; Sodium 228mg.

Grilled Polenta with Gorgonzola

Golden squares of grilled polenta look and taste delicious. Serve spread with any flavourful soft cheese, preferably a blue cheese, or as an accompaniment to soups and salads.

Serves 6–8
350g/12oz/2½ cups
   quick-cook polenta
225g/8oz/1¼ cups Gorgonzola
   cheese, at room temperature

From the storecupboard
15ml/1 tbsp salt

1 Bring 1.5 litres/2½ pints/6¼ cups water to the boil in a large heavy pan. Add the salt. Reduce the heat to a simmer and gradually add the polenta in a fine, steady stream, whisking to incorporate. Change to a wooden spoon and cook, stirring, until the polenta comes away from the sides of the pan.

2 Sprinkle a work surface or large board with a little water. Spread the polenta out on to the surface in a layer 2cm/¾in thick. Allow to cool completely. Preheat the grill (broiler).

3 Cut the polenta into triangles. Grill (broil) on both sides, until hot and speckled with brown. Serve spread with the cheese.

Aubergine, Mint and Couscous Salad

Packets of flavoured couscous are available in most supermarkets – garlic and coriander is especially good for this recipe. Still, it is very simple to make your own flavoured couscous with a good stock and some fresh herbs. Serve with a crisp green salad.

Serves 2
1 large aubergine (eggplant)
115g/4oz packet garlic-and-
   coriander (cilantro)
   flavoured couscous
30ml/2 tbsp chopped fresh mint

From the storecupboard
30ml/2 tbsp olive oil
salt and ground black pepper

1 Preheat the grill (broiler) to high. Cut the aubergine into large chunky pieces and toss them with the olive oil. Season with salt and pepper to taste and spread the aubergine pieces on a non-stick baking sheet. Grill (broil) for 5–6 minutes, turning occasionally, until golden brown.

2 Meanwhile, prepare the couscous according to the instructions on the packet. Stir the grilled aubergine and chopped mint into the couscous, toss thoroughly and serve the dish immediately.

Cook's Tip
Although it looks like a grain, couscous is actually a form of pasta made by steaming and drying cracked durum wheat. The variety that is generally available in supermarkets is quick cooking. Simply place the couscous in a large bowl, add enough boiling water or stock to just cover it and leave covered for 10 minutes or until all the water has been absorbed. Fluff up the grains with a fork and season.

Red Onion and Olive Pissaladière

For a taste of the Mediterranean, try this French-style pizza – it makes a delicious and easy-to-prepare lunch dish or a tasty snack. Cook the sliced red onions slowly until they are caramelized and sweet before piling them into the pastry cases.

Serves 6
500g/1¼lb small red onions,
   thinly sliced
500g/1¼lb puff pastry, thawed
   if frozen
75g/3oz/¾ cup small pitted
   black olives

From the storecupboard
75ml/5 tbsp extra virgin olive oil

1 Preheat the oven to 220°C/425°F/Gas 7. Heat the oil in a large, heavy frying pan and cook the onions gently, stirring frequently, for 15–20 minutes, until they are soft and golden. Season to taste.

2 Roll out the pastry thinly on a floured surface. Cut out a 33cm/13in round and carefully transfer it to a lightly dampened baking sheet.

3 Spread the onions over the pastry in an even layer to within 1cm/½in of the edge. Sprinkle the olives on top.

4 Bake the tart for 20–25 minutes, until the pastry is risen and a deep golden colour. Cut into wedges and serve warm.

Cook's Tip
To prepare the recipe in advance, pile the cooled onions on to the pastry round and chill the pissaladière until you are ready to bake it.

Variation
You can try layering some thin slices of cheese in with the caramelized onions for a change or, alternatively, grate some Parmesan cheese on top.

Grilled Polenta: Energy 252kcal/1052kJ; Protein 8g; Carbohydrate 41.1g, of which sugars 0g; Fat 5.7g, of which saturates 2.5g; Cholesterol 10mg; Calcium 66mg; Fibre 1.2g; Sodium 160mg.
Aubergine Salad: Energy 251kcal/1044kJ; Protein 4.8g; Carbohydrate 32.5g, of which sugars 2g; Fat 12.1g, of which saturates 1.7g; Cholesterol 0mg; Calcium 53mg; Fibre 2g; Sodium 4mg.
Pissaladière: Energy 436kcal/1815kJ; Protein 5.9g; Carbohydrate 37.4g, of which sugars 5.8g; Fat 31.1g, of which saturates 1.5g; Cholesterol 0mg; Calcium 77mg; Fibre 1.5g; Sodium 542mg.

Wild Mushroom and Fontina Tart

You can use any types of wild mushrooms you like in this tart – chanterelles, morels and ceps all have wonderful, distinctive flavours. It makes an impressive vegetarian main course, served with a green salad tossed in an orange and tarragon dressing.

Serves 6

225g/8oz ready-made shortcrust pastry, thawed if frozen
350g/12oz/5 cups mixed wild mushrooms, sliced if large
150g/5oz Fontina cheese, sliced

From the storecupboard
50g/2oz/¼ cup butter
salt and ground black pepper

1 Preheat the oven to 190°C/375°F/Gas 5. Roll out the pastry and use to a line a 23cm/9in loose-bottomed flan tin (tart pan). Chill the pastry for 30 minutes, then bake blind for 15 minutes. Set aside.

2 Heat the butter in a large frying pan until foaming. Add the mushrooms and season with salt and ground black pepper. Cook over a medium heat for 4–5 minutes, moving the mushrooms about and turning them occasionally with a wooden spoon, until golden.

3 Arrange the mushrooms in the cooked pastry case with the Fontina. Return the tart to the oven for 10 minutes, or until the cheese is golden and bubbling. Serve hot.

Cook's Tip
Fontina is a deep golden yellow Italian cheese with a pale brown rind, and lots of little holes permeating the cheese. It melts well, making it a perfect topping for this mushroom tart.

Variation
If wild mushrooms are out of season, use brown cap (cremini) mushrooms, which have a more intense flavour than cultivated varieties. Shiitake mushrooms are also full of flavour.

Mushroom Stroganoff

This creamy mixed mushroom sauce is ideal for a dinner party. Serve it with toasted buckwheat, brown rice or try a mixture of wild rices, and garnish with chopped chives. For best results, choose a variety of different mushrooms – wild mushrooms such as chanterelles, ceps and morels add a delicious flavour and texture to the stroganoff, as well as adding colour and producing a decorative appearance.

Serves 4

900g/2lb mixed mushrooms, cut into bitesize pieces, including
⅔ button (white) mushrooms and ⅓ assorted wild or unusual mushrooms
350ml/12fl oz/1½ cups white wine sauce
250ml/8fl oz/1 cup sour cream

From the storecupboard
25g/1oz/2 tbsp butter
salt and ground black pepper

1 Melt the butter in a pan and quickly cook the mushrooms, in batches, over a high heat, until brown. Transfer the mushrooms to a bowl after cooking each batch.

2 Add the sauce to the juices remaining in the pan and bring to the boil, stirring. Reduce the heat and replace the mushrooms with any juices from the bowl. Stir well and heat for a few seconds, then remove from the heat.

3 Stir the sour cream into the cooked mushroom mixture and season to taste with salt and lots of ground black pepper. Heat through gently for a few seconds, if necessary, then transfer to warm plates and serve immediately.

Cook's Tips
• Wild mushrooms can be found growing in shady areas during late summer, autumn and winter. Take care if you pick your own as certain varieties are poisonous.
• You can use crème fraîche in place of sour cream for a smooth taste in this recipe.

Mushroom Tart: Energy 409kcal/1702kJ; Protein 10.2g; Carbohydrate 21.9g, of which sugars 2.3g; Fat 31g, of which saturates 13.4g; Cholesterol 143mg; Calcium 121mg; Fibre 2.3g; Sodium 199mg.
Mushroom Stroganoff: Energy 408kcal/1685kJ; Protein 6.5g; Carbohydrate 14.3g, of which sugars 6.3g; Fat 34.4g, of which saturates 22.4g; Cholesterol 92mg; Calcium 81mg; Fibre 3.4g; Sodium 88mg.

Mushroom Polenta

This simple recipe uses freshly made polenta, but for an even easier version you can substitute ready-made polenta and slice it straight into the dish, ready for baking. The cheesy mushroom topping is also delicious on toasted herb or sun-dried tomato bread as a light lunch or supper. Any combination of mushrooms will work – try a mixture of button and wild mushrooms as an alternative.

Serves 4
250g/9oz/1½ cups
    quick-cook polenta
400g/14oz brown cap (cremini)
    mushrooms, sliced
175g/6oz/1½ cups grated
    Gruyère cheese

From the storecupboard
50g/2oz/¼ cup butter
salt and ground black pepper

1 Line a 28 x 18cm/11 x 7in shallow baking tin (pan) with baking parchment. Bring 1 litre/1¾ pints/4 cups water with 5ml/1 tsp salt to the boil in a large pan. Add the polenta in a steady stream, stirring constantly. Bring back to the boil, stirring, and cook for approximately 5 minutes, until the polenta is thick and smooth.

2 Turn the polenta into the prepared tin and spread it out into an even layer. Leave to cool.

3 Preheat the oven to 200°C/400°F/Gas 6. Melt the butter in a frying pan and cook the mushrooms for 3–5 minutes, until golden. Season with salt and lots of ground black pepper.

4 Turn out the polenta on to a chopping board. Peel away the baking parchment and cut into large squares.

5 Pile the squares into a shallow, ovenproof dish. Sprinkle with half the cheese, then pile the mushrooms o top and pour over their buttery juices. Sprinkle with the remaining cheese and bake for about 20 minutes, until the cheese is melting and pale golden.

Classic Margherita Pizza

Bought pizza base mixes are a great storecupboard stand-by. A margherita pizza makes a lovely simple supper, but of course you can add any extra toppings you like. Goat's cheese and rocket or artichoke hearts make a great addition – just add them to the pizza after it is cooked.

Serves 2
half a 300g/11oz packet pizza
    base mix, or ready-made base
45ml/3 tbsp ready-made tomato
    and basil sauce
150g/5oz mozzarella, sliced

From the storecupboard
15ml/1 tbsp herb-infused
    olive oil
salt and ground black pepper

1 Make the pizza base mix (if using) according to the instructions on the packet. Brush the base with a little of the olive oil and spread over the tomato and basil sauce, not quite to the edges.

2 Arrange the slices of mozzarella on top of the pizza and bake for 25–30 minutes, or until golden.

3 Drizzle the remaining oil on top of the pizza, season with salt and black pepper and serve immediately, garnished with fresh basil leaves.

Variations
There are endless possibilities for vegetarian pizza toppings. Here are a few to get you started:
• *Fiorentina comprises spinach, thin slices of red onion, an egg and some Gruyère cheese added to the basic margherita.*
• *Quattro formaggi uses four cheeses – Dolcelatte, mozzarella, Gruyère and Parmesan – with some thinly sliced red onion straight on to the pizza base.*
• *Roasted vegetables, such as aubergine (eggplant), red and yellow (bell) peppers, courgette (zucchini) and red onion are delicious on top of a margherita pizza and even better with some goat's cheese crumbled on top.*
• *Black olives give a simple twist to a classic pizza.*

Polenta: Energy 518kcal/2155kJ; Protein 18.9g; Carbohydrate 46.2g, of which sugars 0.3g; Fat 27.2g, of which saturates 16.1g; Cholesterol 69mg; Calcium 334mg; Fibre 2.5g; Sodium 397mg.
Margherita Pizza: Energy 420kcal/1761kJ; Protein 7.6g; Carbohydrate 49.8g, of which sugars 7.8g; Fat 22.6g, of which saturates 2.2g; Cholesterol 2mg; Calcium 133mg; Fibre 3.4g; Sodium 130mg.

Baked Leek and Potato Gratin

Potatoes baked in a creamy cheese sauce make the ultimate comfort dish, whether served as an accompaniment to other dishes or, as here, with plenty of leeks and melted cheese as a main course. When preparing leeks, separate the leaves and rinse them thoroughly under cold running water for a few minutes, as soil and grit often get caught between the layers.

Serves 4–6
900g/2lb medium potatoes, thinly sliced
2 large leeks, trimmed
200g/7oz ripe Brie or Camembert cheese, sliced
450ml/¾ pint/scant 2 cups single (light) cream

From the storecupboard
salt and ground black pepper

1 Preheat the oven to 180°C/350°F/Gas 4. Cook the potatoes in plenty of lightly salted, boiling water for 3 minutes, until slightly softened, then drain. Cut the leeks into 1cm/½in lengths and blanch them in boiling water for 1 minute, until softened, then drain.

2 Turn half the potatoes into a shallow, ovenproof dish and spread them out to the edge. Cover with two-thirds of the leeks, then add the remaining potatoes. Tuck the slices of cheese and the remaining leeks in among the top layer of potatoes. Season and pour the cream over.

3 Bake for 1 hour, until tender and golden. Cover with foil if the top starts to overbrown before the potatoes are tender.

> **Cook's Tip**
> *Brie and Camembert can vary enormously in strength. Some are very mild and others extremely strong. Bear this in mind when selecting a cheese for this dish. A blue cheese, such as Gorgonzola, would bring a rich piquancy to the baked leeks and potatoes, whereas Parmesan would offer a sweet-salt flavour.*

Potato and Onion Tortilla

This deep-set omelette with sliced potatoes and onions is the best-known Spanish tortilla and makes a deliciously simple meal when served with a leafy salad and crusty bread. Tortilla are often made with a variety of ingredients – chopped red or yellow peppers, cooked peas, corn, or grated cheese can all be added to the mixture.

Serves 4–6
800g/1¾lb medium potatoes
2 onions, thinly sliced
6 eggs

From the storecupboard
100ml/3½fl oz/scant ½ cup extra virgin olive oil
salt and ground black pepper

1 Thinly slice the potatoes. Heat 75ml/5 tbsp of the oil in a frying pan and cook the potatoes, turning frequently, for 10 minutes. Add the onions and seasoning, and continue to cook for a further 10 minutes, until the vegetables are tender.

2 Meanwhile, beat the eggs in a large bowl with a little seasoning. Transfer the potatoes and onions into the eggs and mix gently. Leave to stand for 10 minutes.

3 Wipe out the pan with kitchen paper and heat the remaining oil in it. Pour the egg mixture into the pan and spread it out in an even layer. Cover and cook over a very gentle heat for 20 minutes, until the eggs are just set. Serve cut into wedges.

> **Variation**
> *For a fresh and tasty twist on the classic potato and onion tortilla, try adding broad (fava) beans and some chopped fresh herbs to the omelette. Gently cook the potato and onion as you normally would for about 20 minutes in all, without letting it brown. Meanwhile, cook the broad beans in boiling salted water and drain well. When cool enough, remove the broad bean skins, then add the beans to the pan along with 60ml/ 4 tbsp of chopped fresh herbs.*

Leek and Potato: Energy 383kcal/1597kJ; Protein 13.1g; Carbohydrate 28.2g, of which sugars 5.4g; Fat 24.2g, of which saturates 15.4g; Cholesterol 72mg; Calcium 181mg; Fibre 3.3g; Sodium 225mg.
Potato Tortilla: Energy 163kcal/681kJ; Protein 5.8g; Carbohydrate 14.7g, of which sugars 2.9g; Fat 9.5g, of which saturates 1.9g; Cholesterol 127mg; Calcium 32mg; Fibre 1.2g; Sodium 56mg.

Cheesy Leek and Couscous Cake

The tangy flavour of mature Cheddar cheese goes perfectly with the sweet taste of gently fried leeks. The cheese melts into the couscous and helps it stick together, making a firm cake that's easy to cut into wedges. Serve with a crisp green salad.

Serves 4
300g/11oz/1⅔ cups couscous
2 leeks, sliced
200g/7oz/1¾ cups mature
*   (sharp) Cheddar or Monterey*
*   Jack, grated*

From the storecupboard
45ml/3 tbsp olive oil
salt and ground black pepper

1 Put the couscous in a large heatproof bowl and pour over 450ml/¾ pint/scant 2 cups boiling water. Cover and set aside for about 15 minutes, or until all the water has been absorbed.

2 Heat 15ml/1 tbsp of the oil in a 23cm/9in non-stick frying pan. Add the leeks and cook over a medium heat for 4–5 minutes, stirring occasionally, until tender and golden.

3 Remove the leeks with a slotted spoon and stir them into the couscous. Add the grated cheese and some salt and pepper and stir through.

4 Heat the remaining oil in the pan and add the couscous and leek mixture. Pat down firmly to form a cake and cook over a fairly gentle heat for 15 minutes, or until the underside is crisp and golden.

5 Slide the couscous cake on to a plate, then invert it back into the pan to cook the other side. Cook for a further 5–8 minutes, or until golden, then remove from the heat. Slide on to a board and serve cut into wedges.

Variation
There are endless variations on this tangy cake, but use a good melting cheese to bind the cake together. Try using blue cheese and caramelized onions in place of the leeks and Cheddar.

Red Onion and Goat's Cheese Tartlets

These attractive little pastries couldn't be easier to make. Garnish them with fresh thyme sprigs and serve with a selection of salad leaves and a tomato and basil salad for a light lunch or quick supper. A wide variety of different types of goat's cheeses are available – the creamy log-shaped types without a rind are most suitable for these tasty tartlets.

Serves 4
450g/1lb red onions, sliced
425g/15oz packet ready-rolled
*   puff pastry*
115g/4oz/1 cup goat's
*   cheese, cubed*

From the storecupboard
15ml/1 tbsp olive oil
salt and ground black pepper

1 Heat the oil in a large, heavy frying pan, add the onions and cook over a gentle heat for 10 minutes, or until softened, stirring occasionally to prevent them from browning. Add seasoning to taste and cook for a further 2 minutes. Remove the pan from the heat and leave to cool.

2 Preheat the oven to 220°C/425°F/Gas 7. Unroll the puff pastry and using a 15cm/6in plate as a guide, cut out four rounds.

3 Place the pastry rounds on a dampened baking sheet and, using the point of a sharp knife, score a border, 2cm/¾in inside the edge of each pastry round.

4 Divide the onions among the pastry rounds and top with the goat's cheese. Bake for 25–30 minutes until golden brown.

Variation
To make richer-flavoured pastries, ring the changes by spreading the pastry base with red or green pesto, sun-dried tomato paste or tapenade before you top with the goat's cheese and cooked onions.

Cheesy Leek Cake: Energy 475kcal/1973kJ; Protein 18.6g; Carbohydrate 41.4g, of which sugars 2.3g; Fat 25.9g, of which saturates 12.1g; Cholesterol 49mg; Calcium 408mg; Fibre 2.2g; Sodium 364mg.
Red Onion Tartlets: Energy 554kcal/2308kJ; Protein 13.5g; Carbohydrate 48.5g, of which sugars 8g; Fat 36.4g, of which saturates 5.6g; Cholesterol 27mg; Calcium 128mg; Fibre 1.6g; Sodium 506mg.

Roasted Peppers with Halloumi and Pine Nuts

Halloumi cheese is creamy-tasting and has a firm texture and salty flavour that contrasts well with the succulent sweet peppers. This is a good dish to assemble in advance ready to just put in the oven. Halloumi is usually served cooked and lends itself well to barbecuing, frying or grilling. When heated the interior softens like mozzarella cheese, while exterior hardens.

Serves 4
4 red and 2 orange or yellow
    (bell) peppers
250g/9oz halloumi cheese
50g/2oz/½ cup pine nuts

From the storecupboard
60ml/4 tbsp garlic-infused or
    herb-infused olive oil
salt and ground black pepper

1 Preheat the oven to 220°C/425°F/Gas 7. Halve the red peppers, leaving the stalks intact, and discard the seeds. Seed and coarsely chop the orange or yellow peppers.

2 Place the red pepper halves on a baking sheet and fill with the chopped peppers. Drizzle with half the garlic-infused or herb-infused olive oil and bake for 25 minutes, until the edges of the peppers are beginning to char.

3 Dice the cheese and tuck in among the chopped peppers. Sprinkle with the pine nuts and drizzle with the remaining oil. Bake for a further 15 minutes, until well browned. Serve warm with some crusty bread and a green salad.

Cook's Tip
Make your own herb-infused oils by half filling a jar with washed dried fresh herbs. Pour over enough olive oil to cover, then seal the jar and leave in a cool, dark place for 3 days. Strain into a clean jar and discard the herbs.

Tofu and Pepper Kebabs

A simple coating of ground, dry-roasted peanuts pressed on to cubed tofu provides plenty of additional flavour along with the peppers. Use metal or bamboo skewers for the kebabs – if you use bamboo, then soak them in cold water for 30 minutes before using to prevent them from scorching during cooking. The kebabs can also be cooked on a barbecue, if you prefer.

Serves 4
250g/9oz firm tofu
50g/2oz/½ cup
    dry-roasted peanuts
2 red and 2 green (bell) peppers
60ml/4 tbsp sweet chilli
    dipping sauce

From the storecupboard
salt and ground black pepper

1 Pat the tofu dry on kitchen paper and then cut it into small cubes. Grind the peanuts in a blender or food processor and transfer to a plate. Turn the tofu cubes over in the ground nuts to coat on all sides.

2 Preheat the grill (broiler) to moderate. Halve and seed the peppers, and cut them into large chunks. Thread the chunks of pepper on to four large skewers with the tofu cubes and place on a foil-lined grill rack.

3 Grill (broil) the kebabs, turning frequently, for 10–12 minutes, or until the peppers and peanuts are beginning to brown. Transfer the kebabs to plates and serve with the dipping sauce.

Cook's Tip
Tofu, or beancurd, is made from soya milk in a similar way to soft cheese. It is extremely rich in high-quality protein, containing all eight amino acids that are vital for renewal of cells and tissues in the human body. Tofu can be kept in the refrigerator in an airtight container for up to 1 week. Firm tofu, as used in this recipe, should be covered in water, which should be changed daily, to keep it completely fresh for up to a week.

Roasted Peppers: Energy 506kcal/2099kJ; Protein 18.4g; Carbohydrate 32.5g, of which sugars 31g; Fat 34.3g, of which saturates 11.3g; Cholesterol 36mg; Calcium 268mg; Fibre 8.3g; Sodium 267mg.
Tofu Kebabs: Energy 187kcal/778kJ; Protein 10.2g; Carbohydrate 16.8g, of which sugars 15.1g; Fat 9.1g, of which saturates 1.6g; Cholesterol 0mg; Calcium 342mg; Fibre 3.7g; Sodium 214mg.

Tomato and Tapenade Tarts

These delicious individual tarts look and taste fantastic, despite the fact that they demand very little time or effort. The mascarpone cheese topping melts as it cooks to make a smooth, creamy sauce. Cherry tomatoes have a delicious sweet flavour with a low acidity, but plum tomatoes or vine-ripened tomatoes are also suitable for these tarts and will give delicious results. Red pesto can be used instead of the tapenade if you prefer a subtler flavour.

Serves 4

500g/1¼ lb puff pastry, thawed if frozen
60ml/4 tbsp black or green olive tapenade
500g/1¼ lb cherry tomatoes
90g/3½ oz/scant ½ cup mascarpone cheese

From the storecupboard

salt and ground black pepper

1 Preheat the oven to 220°C/425°F/Gas 7. Lightly grease a large baking sheet and sprinkle it with water. Roll out the pastry on a lightly floured surface and cut out four 16cm/6½in rounds, using a bowl or small plate as a guide.

2 Transfer the pastry rounds to the prepared baking sheet. Using the tip of a sharp knife, mark a shallow cut 1cm/½in in from the edge of each round to form a rim.

3 Reserve half the tapenade and spread the rest over the pastry rounds, keeping the paste inside the marked rim. Cut half the tomatoes in half. Pile all the tomatoes, whole and halved, on the pastry, again keeping them inside the rim. Season lightly.

4 Bake for 20 minutes, until the pastry is well risen and golden. Dot with the remaining tapenade. Spoon a little mascarpone on the centre of the tomatoes and season with black pepper. Bake for a further 10 minutes, until the mascarpone has melted to make a sauce. Serve the tarts warm.

Cheese and Tomato Soufflés

Using a ready-made cheese sauce takes the effort out of soufflé making. The key to success when making soufflés is to whisk the egg whites thoroughly to incorporate as much air as possible. During the cooking time don't open the oven door – the cold draught could cause the delicate mixture to collapse.

Serves 6

350g/12oz tub fresh cheese sauce
50g/2oz sun-dried tomatoes in olive oil, drained, plus 10ml/2 tsp of the oil
130g/4½ oz/1⅓ cups grated Parmesan cheese
4 large (US extra large) eggs, separated

From the storecupboard

salt and ground black pepper

1 Preheat the oven to 200°C/400°F/Gas 6. Turn the cheese sauce into a bowl. Thinly slice the sun-dried tomatoes and add to the bowl with 90g/3½oz/generous 1 cup of the Parmesan, the egg yolks and seasoning. Stir until well combined.

2 Brush the base and sides of six 200ml/7fl oz/scant 1 cup ramekins with the oil and then coat the insides of the dishes with half the remaining cheese, tilting them until evenly covered.

3 Whisk the egg whites in a clean bowl until stiff. Use a large metal spoon to stir one-quarter of the egg whites into the sauce, then fold in the remainder. Spoon the mixture into the prepared dishes and sprinkle with the remaining Parmesan cheese. Place on a baking sheet and bake for 15–18 minutes, until well risen and golden. Serve the soufflés as soon as you remove them from the oven.

> **Cook's Tip**
> *To make a cheese sauce, melt 25g/1oz/2 tbsp butter in a pan and stir in 25g/1oz/¼ cup plain (all-purpose) flour. Remove from the heat, then gradually add 200ml/7fl oz/scant 1 cup milk. Stir, return to heat and bring to the boil, stirring. Take off the heat and add 115g/4oz/1 cup grated Cheddar cheese.*

Tomato Tarts: Energy 543kcal/2269kJ; Protein 10.2g; Carbohydrate 50.8g, of which sugars 6.2g; Fat 35.9g, of which saturates 2.4g; Cholesterol 9mg; Calcium 91mg; Fibre 1.7g; Sodium 736mg.
Cheese Soufflés: Energy 328kcal/1364kJ; Protein 20g; Carbohydrate 6.2g, of which sugars 3g; Fat 24.7g, of which saturates 13.6g; Cholesterol 184mg; Calcium 497mg; Fibre 0.2g; Sodium 473mg.

Mixed Bean and Tomato Chilli

Here, mixed beans, fiery red chilli and plenty of freshly chopped coriander are simmered in a tomato sauce to make a delicious vegetarian chilli. Always a popular dish for a quick and easy lunch, chilli can be served with a variety of accompaniments – choose from baked potatoes, baked rice, crusty bread or tortillas. Garnish with slices of tomato, chopped celery or sweet pepper and top with natural yogurt.

Serves 4

*400g/14oz jar ready-made
    tomato and herb sauce*
*2 x 400g/14oz cans mixed
    beans, drained and rinsed*
1 fresh red chilli
*large handful of fresh
    coriander (cilantro)*

From the storecupboard
salt and ground black pepper

1 Pour the ready-made tomato sauce and mixed beans into a pan. Seed and thinly slice the chilli, then add it to the pan. Reserve a little of the coriander, chop the remainder and add it to the pan.

2 Bring the mixture to the boil, reduce the heat, cover and simmer gently for 10 minutes. Stir the mixture occasionally and add a dash of water if the sauce starts to dry out.

3 Ladle the chilli into warmed individual serving bowls and top with a spoonful of yogurt to serve.

Cook's Tip
To make a tomato and herb sauce, heat 15ml/1 tbsp olive oil in a pan, add 1 chopped onion and fry for 3–4 minutes until soft. Add 1 chopped garlic clove and cook for about 1 minute more. Pour in 400g/14oz chopped tomatoes and stir in 15ml/ 1 tbsp tomato purée (paste). Add 30ml/2 tbsp dried oregano or dried mixed herbs and simmer for about 15 minutes, until thickened. Season with salt and pepper.

Spicy Chickpea Samosas

A blend of crushed chickpeas and coriander sauce makes an interesting alternative to the more familiar vegetable fillings in these moreish little pastries. Garnish with fresh coriander leaves and finely sliced onion and serve with a simple, but delicious, dip made from Greek yogurt and chopped fresh mint leaves.

Makes 18

*2 x 400g/14oz cans chickpeas,
    drained and rinsed*
*120ml/4fl oz/½ cup hara masala
    or coriander (cilantro) sauce*
275g/10oz filo pastry

From the storecupboard
*60ml/4 tbsp chilli-and-garlic
    flavoured oil*
salt and ground black pepper

1 Preheat the oven to 220°C/425°F/Gas 7. Process half the chickpeas to a paste in a food processor. Put the paste into a bowl and add the whole chickpeas, the hara masala or coriander sauce, and a little salt. Mix until well combined.

2 Lay a sheet of filo pastry on a work surface and cut into three strips. Brush the strips with a little of the oil. Place a dessertspoon of the filling at one end of a strip. Turn one corner diagonally over the filling to meet the long edge. Continue folding the filling and the pastry along the length of the strip, keeping the triangular shape. Transfer to a baking sheet and repeat with the remaining filling and pastry.

3 Brush the pastries with any remaining oil and bake for 15 minutes, until the pastry is golden. Cool before serving.

Cook's Tip
To make chilli oil, add several dried chillis to a bottle of olive oil and leave to infuse (steep) for about 2 weeks before checking. If the flavour hasn't infused sufficiently, leave for a further week before using. The chillies can be left in the bottle as they give a decorative effect. Garlic oil is made in the same way with peeled garlic cloves, but remove the cloves once infused.

Bean Chilli: Energy 309kcal/1302kJ; Protein 16.7g; Carbohydrate 43.7g, of which sugars 14.1g; Fat 8.7g, of which saturates 4.2g; Cholesterol 18mg; Calcium 193mg; Fibre 12.4g; Sodium 1202mg.
Chickpea Samosas: Energy 119kcal/499kJ; Protein 4.1g; Carbohydrate 13.7g, of which sugars 0.4g; Fat 5.7g, of which saturates 0.8g; Cholesterol 0mg; Calcium 36mg; Fibre 2.2g; Sodium 99mg

Creamy Red Lentil Dhal

This spicy dish makes a tasty and satisfying winter-warming vegetarian supper. Serve with naan bread, coconut cream and fresh coriander leaves. The coconut cream gives the dish a really rich taste.

Serves 4
500g/1¼lb/2 cups red lentils
15ml/1 tbsp hot curry paste

From the storecupboard
15ml/1 tbsp sunflower oil
salt and ground black pepper

1 Heat the oil in a large pan and add the lentils. Fry for 1–2 minutes, stirring continuously, then stir in the curry paste and 600ml/1 pint/2½ cups boiling water.

2 Bring the mixture to the boil, then reduce the heat to a gentle simmer. Cover the pan and cook for 15 minutes, stirring occasionally, until the lentils are tender and the mixture has thickened.

3 Season the dhal with plenty of salt and ground black pepper to taste, and serve piping hot.

Cook's Tip
The orange-coloured red split lentils are the most familiar variety. They cook in just 20 minutes, eventually forming a thick purée. They are very low in fat and have an impressive range of health benefits, including the reduction of cholesterol and aiding bowel function. They are richer in protein than most pulses, too.

Variation
The Indian naan bread is easy to find in supermarkets and is available plain or flavoured with herbs and spices, such as garlic and coriander (cilantro). You can also buy the delicious Peshwari naan filled with coconut and sultanas (golden raisins). The flatbread chapati is less heavy and would make a good alternative.

Spiced Lentils

The combination of Puy lentils, tomatoes and cheese is widely used in Mediterranean cooking. The tang of feta cheese complements the slightly earthy flavour of the attractive dark lentils wonderfully. Serve this richly comforting dish with a big hunk of crusty bread.

Serves 4
250g/9oz/1½ cups Puy lentils
200g/7oz feta cheese
75ml/5 tbsp sun-dried tomato purée (paste)
small handful of fresh chervil or flat leaf parsley, chopped, plus extra to garnish

From the storecupboard
salt and ground black pepper

1 Place the lentils in a heavy pan with 600ml/1 pint/2½ cups water. Bring to the boil, reduce the heat and cover the pan. Simmer gently for at least 20 minutes, until the lentils are just tender and most of the water has been absorbed.

2 Crumble half the feta cheese into the pan. Add the sun-dried tomato purée, chopped chervil or flat leaf parsley and a little salt and ground black pepper. Heat through for 1 minute.

3 Transfer the lentil mixture and juices to warmed plates or bowls. Crumble the remaining feta cheese on top and sprinkle with the fresh herbs to garnish. Serve hot.

Cook's Tip
True Puy lentils come from the region of France, Le Puy, which has a unique climate and volcanic soil in which they thrive.

Variations
• Any of the more robust fresh herbs could be used with this dish. Try basil, oregano, marjoram or thyme.
• You could also vary the cheese. Ricotta salata, the Italian salted ricotta, would be an option.
• Really spice this dish up with a little chilli powder or paprika.

Creamy Lentil Dhal: Energy 455kcal/1929kJ; Protein 30.1g; Carbohydrate 71.3g, of which sugars 3g; Fat 7.5g, of which saturates 1g; Cholesterol 0mg; Calcium 86mg; Fibre 6.9g; Sodium 61mg.
Spiced Lentils: Energy 339kcal/1427kJ; Protein 23.7g; Carbohydrate 38.6g, of which sugars 4.9g; Fat 11g, of which saturates 7g; Cholesterol 35mg; Calcium 221mg; Fibre 3.7g; Sodium 788mg.

Roast Acorn Squash with Spinach and Gorgonzola

Roasting squash brings out its sweetness, here offset by tangy cheese. Acorn squash has been used here, but any type of squash will give delicious results.

Serves 4

4 acorn squash
250g/9oz baby spinach
   leaves, washed
200g/7oz Gorgonzola
   cheese, sliced

From the storecupboard
45ml/3 tbsp garlic-infused olive oil
salt and ground black pepper

1 Preheat the oven to 190°C/375°F/Gas 5. Cut the tops off the squash, and scoop out and discard the seeds. Place the squash, cut side up, in a roasting pan and drizzle with 30ml/ 2 tbsp of the oil. Season with salt and pepper and bake for 30–40 minutes, or until tender.

2 Heat the remaining oil in a large frying pan and add the spinach leaves. Cook over a medium heat for 2–3 minutes, until the leaves are just wilted. Season with salt and pepper and divide between the squash halves.

3 Top with the Gorgonzola and return to the oven for 10 minutes, or until the cheese has melted. Season with ground black pepper and serve.

Cook's Tip
There are many different types of squash, coming in all different shapes and sizes. They have a rich sweet flesh that can be used in both sweet and savoury dishes. Acorn squash has a slightly dry texture and a large seed cavity perfect for stuffing. Squash contain high levels of antioxidant, which are believed to reduce the risk of certain cancers. You could use a pumpkin in place of acorn squash, but be sure to choose a small one as they have the sweetest, less fibrous flesh.

Stuffed Baby Squash

It is worth making the most of baby squash while they are in season. Use any varieties you can find and do not worry too much about choosing vegetables of uniform size, as an assortment of different types and sizes looks attractive. The baked vegetables can easily be shared out at the table. Serve with warm crusty white bread and a ready-made spicy tomato sauce for a hearty autumn supper.

Serves 4

4 small squash, each about
   350g/12oz
200g/7oz/1 cup mixed wild and
   basmati rice
150g/5oz/1¼ cups grated
   Gruyère cheese

From the storecupboard
60ml/4 tbsp chilli and garlic oil
salt and ground black pepper

1 Preheat the oven to 190°C/375°F/Gas 5. Pierce the squash in several places with the tip of a knife. Bake for 30 minutes, until the squash are tender. Leave until cool enough to handle.

2 Meanwhile, cook the rice in salted, boiling water for 12 minutes, until tender, then drain. Slice a lid off the top of each squash and scoop out and discard the seeds. Scoop out and chop the flesh.

3 Heat the oil in a frying pan and cook the chopped squash for 5 minutes. Reserve 60ml/4 tbsp of the cheese, add the remainder to the pan with the rice and a little salt. Mix well.

4 Pile the mixture into the squash shells and place in a dish. Sprinkle with the remaining cheese and bake for 20 minutes.

Cook's Tip
Serve this hearty flavourful dish with some warm sun-dried tomato or olive bread and some spicy tomato salsa or home-made chutney.

Acorn Squash: Energy 310kcal/1285kJ; Protein 14.6g; Carbohydrate 9.3g, of which sugars 7.3g; Fat 24g, of which saturates 11.2g; Cholesterol 38mg; Calcium 459mg; Fibre 5.1g; Sodium 698mg.
Stuffed Squash: Energy 483kcal/2011kJ; Protein 15.9g; Carbohydrate 48.2g, of which sugars 6.4g; Fat 24.3g, of which saturates 10.1g; Cholesterol 36mg; Calcium 396mg; Fibre 3.8g; Sodium 271mg.

Aubergines with Cheese Sauce

This wonderfully simple dish of aubergines in cheese sauce is delicious hot and the perfect dish to assemble ahead of time ready for baking at the last minute. Kashkaval cheese is particularly good in this recipe – it is a hard yellow cheese made from sheep's milk and is originally from the Balkans. Serve with lots of crusty bread to mop up the delicious aubergine-flavoured cheese sauce.

Serves 4–6
2 large aubergines (eggplants), cut into 5mm/¼in thick slices
400g/14oz/3½ cups grated cheese, such as kashkaval, Gruyère, or a mixture of Parmesan and Cheddar
600ml/1 pint/2½ cups savoury white sauce or béchamel sauce

From the storecupboard
about 60ml/4 tbsp olive oil
salt and ground black pepper

1 Layer the aubergine slices in a bowl or colander, sprinkling each layer with salt, and leave to drain for at least 30 minutes. Rinse well, then pat dry with kitchen paper.

2 Heat the oil in a frying pan, then cook the aubergine slices until golden brown on both sides. Remove from the pan and set aside.

3 Preheat the oven to 180°C/350°F/Gas 4. Mix most of the grated cheese into the savoury white or béchamel sauce, reserving a little to sprinkle on top of the finished dish.

4 Arrange a layer of the aubergines in an ovenproof dish, then pour over some sauce. Repeat, ending with sauce. Sprinkle with the reserved cheese. Bake for 35–40 minutes until golden.

> **Cook's Tip**
> Serve this dish with a nice leafy green salad and plenty of crusty white bread. The chewy Italian olive oil bread, ciabatta, would make a good choice.

Tomato and Aubergine Gratin

This colourful dish from the Mediterranean makes a filling main meal or can be served as an accompaniment. If you prefer, thinly sliced courgettes (zucchini) can be used instead of the aubergines. Grill the courgettes for 10–15 minutes. Choose plum tomatoes if you can – they have fewer seeds than most round tomatoes, so are less watery and are ideal for cooking.

Serves 4–6
2 medium aubergines (eggplants), about 500g/1¼ lb
400g/14oz ripe tomatoes, sliced
40g/1½ oz/½ cup freshly grated Parmesan cheese

From the storecupboard
90ml/6 tbsp olive oil
salt and ground black pepper

1 Preheat the grill (broiler) to medium-high. Thinly slice the aubergines and arrange them in a single layer on a foil-lined grill rack.

2 Brush the aubergine slices with some of the oil and grill (broil) for 15–20 minutes, turning once, until golden on both sides. Brush the second side with more oil after turning the slices.

3 Preheat the oven to 200°C/400°F/Gas 6. Toss the aubergine and tomato slices together in a bowl with a little seasoning, then pile them into a shallow, ovenproof dish. Drizzle with any remaining olive oil and then sprinkle with the grated Parmesan cheese.

4 Bake for 20 minutes, until the cheese is golden and the vegetables are hot. Serve the gratin immediately.

> **Variation**
> Instead of using fresh tomatoes in this recipe, you can layer the aubergine and Parmesan with passata (bottled strained tomatoes) and artichoke hearts.

Aubergines: Energy 535kcal/2219kJ; Protein 24.3g; Carbohydrate 13.9g, of which sugars 7.5g; Fat 41.3g, of which saturates 19.8g; Cholesterol 78mg; Calcium 705mg; Fibre 2.1g; Sodium 957mg.
Tomato Gratin: Energy 101kcal/420kJ; Protein 3.7g; Carbohydrate 3.5g, of which sugars 3.4g; Fat 8.1g, of which saturates 2.3g; Cholesterol 7mg; Calcium 91mg; Fibre 2g; Sodium 80mg.

Tagliatelle with Vegetable Ribbons

Narrow strips of courgette and carrot mingle well with tagliatelle to resemble coloured pasta. Serve as a side dish, or sprinkle with freshly grated Parmesan cheese for a light appetizer or main course. Flavoured oils, such as garlic (used here), herbs or chilli, are widely available and are a quick way of adding flavour to pasta.

Serves 4
2 large courgettes (zucchini)
2 large carrots
250g/9oz fresh egg tagliatelle

From the storecupboard
60ml/4 tbsp garlic-flavoured olive oil
salt and ground black pepper

I With a vegetable peeler, cut the courgettes and carrots into long thin ribbons. Bring a large pan of salted water to the boil, then add the courgette and carrot ribbons. Bring the water back to the boil and boil for 30 seconds, drain and set aside.

2 Cook the tagliatelle according to the instructions on the packet. Drain the pasta and return it to the pan. Add the vegetable ribbons, garlic-flavoured oil and seasoning and toss over a medium to high heat until the pasta and vegetables are glistening with oil. Serve the pasta immediately.

Cook's Tip
To make your own herb oils, half fill a jar with washed and dried fresh herbs. Pour over olive oil to cover, then seal the jar and store in cool, dark place for 3 days. Strain the oil into a clean jar and discard the herbs.

Variation
Other types of long pasta are suitable for this dish: try the slightly narrower fettucine, or pappardelle, the broad ribbon noodles with wavy edges.

Spaghetti with Raw Tomato and Ricotta Sauce

This wonderfully simple uncooked sauce goes well with many different kinds of freshly cooked pasta, both long strands such as spaghetti, tagliatelle or linguine, and short shapes such as macaroni, rigatoni or penne. It is always at its best in summer when made with rich, sweet plum tomatoes that have ripened on the vine in the sun and have their fullest flavour.

Serves 4
500g/1¼ lb ripe Italian plum tomatoes
350g/12oz dried spaghetti or pasta of your choice
115g/4oz ricotta salata cheese, diced

From the storecupboard
75ml/5 tbsp garlic-flavoured olive oil
salt and ground black pepper

I Coarsely chop the plum tomatoes, removing the cores and as many of the seeds as you can.

2 Put the tomatoes and oil in a bowl, adding salt and pepper to taste, and stir well. Cover and leave at room temperature for 1–2 hours to let the flavours mingle.

3 Cook the spaghetti or your chosen pasta according to the packet instructions, then drain well.

4 Taste the sauce to check the seasoning before tossing it with the hot pasta. Sprinkle with the cheese and serve immediately.

Cook's Tips
• *The Italian cheese, ricotta salata, is a salted and dried version of ricotta cheese. If it is not available, you can substitute it with the ubiquitous feta cheese in this dish.*
• *Add some plump and juicy black olives; not only are they delicious, but they help to reduce cholesterol and thereby reduce the risk of heart attack.*

Tagliatelle: Energy 397kcal/1663kJ; Protein 11.5g; Carbohydrate 52.4g, of which sugars 8.3g; Fat 17.1g, of which saturates 3.3g; Cholesterol 19mg; Calcium 80mg; Fibre 4.8g; Sodium 127mg.
Spaghetti and Ricotta: Energy 496kcal/2087kJ; Protein 14g; Carbohydrate 69.6g, of which sugars 7.7g; Fat 19.9g, of which saturates 4.9g; Cholesterol 12mg; Calcium 31mg; Fibre 3.8g; Sodium 14mg.

Risotto with Asparagus

Fresh farm asparagus only has a short season, so make the most of it with this elegant risotto.

Serves 3–4
225g/8oz fresh asparagus
750ml/1¼ pints/3 cups
  vegetable stock

1 small onion, finely chopped
275g/10oz/1½ cups risotto rice,
  such as arborio or carnaroli
75g/3oz/1 cup freshly grated
  Parmesan cheese, to serve

From the storecupboard
65g/2½oz/5 tbsp butter
salt and ground black pepper

1 Bring a pan of water to the boil. Cut off any woody pieces on the ends of the asparagus stalks, peel the lower portions, then cook in the water for 5 minutes. Drain the asparagus, reserving the cooking water, refresh under cold water and drain again. Cut the asparagus diagonally into 4cm/1¼in pieces. Keep the tip and next-highest sections separate from the stalks.

2 Place the vegetable stock in a pan and add 450ml/¾ pint/ scant 2 cups of the asparagus cooking water. Heat to simmering point and keep it hot.

3 Melt two-thirds of the butter in a large, heavy pan or deep frying pan. Add the onion and fry until it is soft and golden. Stir in all the asparagus except the top two sections. Cook for 2–3 minutes. Add the rice and cook for 1–2 minutes, mixing well to coat it with butter.

4 Stir in a ladleful of the hot liquid. Using a wooden spoon, stir until the stock has been absorbed. Gradually add the remaining stock, a little at a time, allowing the rice to absorb the liquid before adding more, and stirring all the time.

5 After 10 minutes, add the remaining asparagus sections. Continue to cook as before, for about 15 minutes, until the rice is *al dente* and the risotto is creamy.

6 Off the heat, stir in the remaining butter and the Parmesan, if using. Season and serve.

Sultan's Chickpea Pilaff

A classic buttery pilaff, fit for a sultan according to Turkish legend, this dish makes a satisfying supper or can be served as the perfect accompaniment to almost any main course.

Serves 4
50g/2oz/⅓ cup dried chickpeas,
  soaked in cold water overnight

1 onion, chopped
225g/8oz/generous 1 cup
  long grain rice, well rinsed
  and drained
600ml/1 pint/2½ cups vegetable
  stock or water

From the storecupboard
30ml/2 tbsp butter
15ml/1 tbsp olive or sunflower oil
salt and ground black pepper

1 Drain the chickpeas, transfer them into a pan and fill the pan with plenty of cold water. Bring to the boil and boil for 1 minute, then lower the heat and partially cover the pan. Simmer the chickpeas for about 45 minutes, or until tender. Drain, rinse well under cold running water and remove any loose skins.

2 Melt the butter with the oil in a heavy pan, stir in the onion and cook until it softens. Add the rice and chickpeas and cover with the water or stock. Season with salt and pepper and bring to the boil. Lower the heat, partially cover the pan and simmer for 10–12 minutes, until almost all of the water has been absorbed.

3 Turn off the heat, cover the pan with a dish towel and put the lid tightly on top. Leave the rice to steam for 10 minutes, then fluff up with a fork before serving.

Cook's Tip
Like all rice dishes, this Sultan's Chickpea Pilaff is best made with a well-flavoured vegetable stock. You can make your own in advance and store in the refrigerator for up to three days or in the freezer for up to six months. If you do not have time to make fresh stock, use a carton or can of good quality stock.

Asparagus Risotto: Energy 467kcal/1940kJ; Protein 14.2g; Carbohydrate 56.1g, of which sugars 1.2g; Fat 20.2g, of which saturates 12.4g; Cholesterol 53mg; Calcium 256mg; Fibre 1g; Sodium 304mg.
Chickpea Pilaff: Energy 328kcal/1368kJ; Protein 7.1g; Carbohydrate 52.3g, of which sugars 1.2g; Fat 9.9g, of which saturates 4.4g; Cholesterol 16mg; Calcium 36mg; Fibre 1.6g; Sodium 51mg.

VEGETABLES AND SIDE DISHES

Asparagus with Lemon Sauce

Sometimes less is more: here a simple egg and lemon dressing brings out the best in asparagus. Serve this asparagus dish as an accompaniment to your favourite main dish. Alternatively, enjoy it for a light supper, with crusty bread and butter to mop up the delicious lemony juices.

Serves 4

675g/1½ lb asparagus, tough ends removed, and tied in a bundle
15ml/1 tbsp cornflour (cornstarch)
2 egg yolks
juice of 1½ lemons

From the storecupboard
salt and ground black pepper

1 Cook the bundle of asparagus in a tall pan of lightly salted, boiling water for 7–10 minutes.

2 Drain well and arrange the asparagus in a serving dish. Reserve 200ml/7fl oz/scant 1 cup of the cooking liquid.

3 Blend the cornflour with the cooled, reserved cooking liquid and place in a pan. Bring to the boil, stirring constantly, and cook over a gentle heat until the sauce thickens slightly. Remove the pan from the heat and leave to cool.

4 Beat the egg yolks with the lemon juice and stir into the cooled sauce. Cook over a low heat, stirring constantly, until the sauce is thick. Be careful not to overheat the sauce or it may curdle. As soon as the sauce has thickened, remove the pan from the heat and continue stirring for 1 minute. Taste and season with salt. Leave the sauce to cool slightly.

5 Stir the cooled lemon sauce, then pour a little over the cooked asparagus. Cover and chill in the refrigerator for at least 2 hours before serving with the rest of the sauce.

Cook's Tip
For a slightly less tangy sauce, add a little caster (superfine) sugar with the salt in step 4.

Braised Lettuce and Peas with Spring Onions

This light vegetable dish is based on the classic French method of braising peas with lettuce and spring onions in butter. A sprinkling of chopped fresh mint makes a fresh, flavoursome and extremely pretty garnish. Other legumes such as broad beans, mangetouts, edamame beans and sugar snap peas can be used instead of peas to create a delicious variation.

Serves 4

4 Little Gem (Bibb) lettuces, halved lengthways
2 bunches spring onions (scallions), trimmed
400g/14oz shelled peas (about 1kg/2¼ lb in pods)

From the storecupboard
50g/2oz/¼ cup butter
salt and ground black pepper

1 Melt half the butter in a wide, heavy pan over a low heat. Add the lettuces and spring onions.

2 Turn the vegetables in the butter, then sprinkle in salt and plenty of ground black pepper. Cover, and cook the vegetables very gently for 5 minutes, stirring once.

3 Add the peas and turn them in the buttery juices. Pour in 120ml/4fl oz/½ cup water, then cover and cook over a gentle heat for a further 5 minutes. Uncover and increase the heat to reduce the liquid to a few tablespoons.

4 Stir in the remaining butter and adjust the seasoning. Transfer to a warmed serving dish and serve immediately.

Variation
For a different texture, you can braise about 250g/9oz baby carrots or baby corn with the lettuce.

Asparagus with Lemon: Energy 96kcal/399kJ; Protein 6.4g; Carbohydrate 9.4g, of which sugars 5.8g; Fat 3.8g, of which saturates 1g; Cholesterol 101mg; Calcium 59mg; Fibre 2.9g; Sodium 8mg.
Lettuce and Peas: Energy 161kcal/670kJ; Protein 9.1g; Carbohydrate 15.9g, of which sugars 6.8g; Fat 7.4g, of which saturates 3.7g; Cholesterol 13mg; Calcium 73mg; Fibre 6.5g; Sodium 47mg.

Braised Swiss Chard

Swiss chard (also known as spinach beet) is less well known than spinach. It makes two tasty meals: on the first day, cook the leaves; the next day cook the stalks in the same way as asparagus and serve with cream or a white sauce. Alternatively, you can serve both together, the green leaves heaped up in the middle of a serving dish with the stems around them.

Serves 4
900g/2lb Swiss chard or spinach
a little freshly grated nutmeg

From the storecupboard
15g/½oz/1 tbsp butter
sea salt and ground black pepper

1 Remove the stalks from the Swiss chard or spinach (and reserve the chard stalks, if you like – see Cook's Tip). Wash the leaves well and lift straight into a lightly greased heavy pan; the water clinging to the leaves will be all that is needed for cooking.

2 Cover with a tight-fitting lid and cook over a medium heat for about 3–5 minutes, or until the leaves are just tender, shaking the pan occasionally.

3 Drain well, add the butter and nutmeg, and season to taste. When the butter has melted, toss it into the Swiss chard and serve immediately.

Cook's Tip
To cook the stalks of Swiss chard, trim the bases, wash them well and tie in bundles like asparagus. Place in a pan of boiling water, with a squeeze of lemon juice added, and cook for about 20 minutes, or until tender but still slightly crisp. Drain and serve the chard stalks with a white sauce or simply pour over 30ml/2 tbsp fresh single (light) cream, heat through gently, season and serve.

Crispy Cabbage

This quick side dish is deliciously crunchy. The crinkly Savoy cabbage looks especially pretty cooked this way, as it keeps its verdant colour beautifully.

Serves 4–6
1 medium green or small white cabbage

From the storecupbaord
30–45ml/2–3 tbsp oil
salt and ground black pepper

1 Remove any coarse outside leaves from the cabbage and also the central rib from the larger leaves. Shred the remaining leaves finely. Wash well under cold running water, shake well and pat with kitchen paper to dry.

2 Heat a wok or wide-based flameproof casserole over a fairly high heat. Heat the oil and add the cabbage. Stir-fry for 2–3 minutes, or until it is just cooked but still crunchy. Season and serve immediately.

Cook's Tip
Take care not to overcook the cabbage as not only will it lose its crunchy texture and bright green colour (in the case of Savoy), but it will also lose some of the health-giving properties. Studies show that, when eaten more than once a week, cabbage can reduce the likelihood of colon cancer in men by about 65 per cent.

Variation
For crispy cabbage with a mustard dressing, whisk 45ml/3 tbsp light olive oil into 5ml/1 tsp wholegrain mustard in a bowl. When blended completely, whisk in 15ml/1 tbsp white wine vinegar. The dressing should begin to thicken. Season the mustard dressing to taste with 5ml/1 tsp agave syrup, a little salt and plenty of ground black pepper. Set aside while cooking the cabbage. Toss the cooked cabbage in the mustard dressing and serve immediately.

Braised Swiss Chard: Energy 84kcal/347kJ; Protein 6.3g; Carbohydrate 3.6g, of which sugars 3.4g; Fat 4.9g, of which saturates 2.2g; Cholesterol 8mg; Calcium 383mg; Fibre 4.7g; Sodium 338mg.
Crispy Cabbage: Energy 54kcal/224kJ; Protein 1.9g; Carbohydrate 4.6g, of which sugars 4.5g; Fat 3.2g, of which saturates 0.5g; Cholesterol 0mg; Calcium 59mg; Fibre 2.7g; Sodium 6mg.

Colcannon

This traditional Irish dish is particularly associated with Hallowe'en, when it is likely to be made with curly kale and would have a ring hidden in it – predicting marriage during the coming year for the person who found it. However, it is also served throughout the winter, and green cabbage is more often used.

Serves 3–4 as a main dish, 6–8 as an accompaniment

450g/1lb potatoes, peeled and boiled
450g/1lb curly kale or cabbage, cooked
milk, if necessary
1 large onion, finely chopped

From the storecupboard

50g/2oz/2 tbsp butter, plus extra for serving
salt and ground black pepper

1 Mash the boiled potatoes. Chop the cooked kale or cabbage, add it to the potatoes and mix. Stir in a little milk if the mash is too stiff.

2 Melt a little butter in a frying pan over a medium heat and add the onion. Cook until softened. Remove and mix well with the potato and kale or cabbage.

3 Add the remainder of the butter to the hot pan. When very hot, turn the potato mixture into the pan and spread it out. Fry until brown, then cut it roughly into pieces and continue frying until they are crisp and brown.

4 Serve in bowls or as a side dish, with plenty of butter.

> **Cook's Tips**
> • Although it is often eaten as a dish in its own right, colcannon also makes an excellent accompaniment to many of your favourite main courses.
> • Other ingredients may be added to the colcannon to ring the changes, such as cream instead of milk, leeks, chives, spring onions or wild garlic in place of the onion.

Tomato with Marinated Peppers and Oregano

The Portuguese usually prepare this refreshing appetizer with home-grown tomatoes for maximum flavour and sweetness. They combine superbly with marinated peppers, which, because they have been well roasted before soaking, are sweeter and more digestible than raw ones.

Serves 4–6

2 marinated (bell) peppers, drained
6 ripe tomatoes, sliced
15ml/1 tbsp chopped fresh oregano
30ml/2 tbsp white wine vinegar

From the storecupboard

75ml/5 tbsp olive oil
sea salt

1 If the marinated peppers are in large pieces, cut them into strips. Arrange the tomato slices and pepper strips on a serving dish, sprinkle with the oregano and season to taste with sea salt.

2 Whisk together the olive oil and vinegar in a jug (pitcher) and pour the dressing over the salad. Serve immediately or cover and chill in the refrigerator until required.

> **Cook's Tips**
> • Marinated (bell) peppers are widely available in jars, often labelled as pimentos. However, they are much tastier when prepared yourself. To do this, wrap one green and one red pepper in foil and place on a baking sheet. Cook in a preheated oven at 180°C/350°F/Gas 4, or under a preheated grill (broiler), turning occasionally, for 20–30 minutes, until tender. Unwrap and when cool, peel the peppers, then halve and seed. Cut the flesh into strips and pack into a screw-top jar. Add olive oil to cover, close and store in the refrigerator for up to 6 days.
> • You can preserve marinated peppers by cooking them in a closed jar in boiling water for about 30 minutes. They can then be kept for approximately 6 weeks.

Colcannon: Energy 306kcal/1281kJ; Protein 5.4g; Carbohydrate 40.6g, of which sugars 13.6g; Fat 14.6g, of which saturates 8.8g; Cholesterol 36mg; Calcium 104mg; Fibre 5.9g; Sodium 127mg.
Tomatoes and Peppers: Energy 119kcal/494kJ; Protein 1.4g; Carbohydrate 6.9g, of which sugars 6.7g; Fat 9.7g, of which saturates 1.5g; Cholesterol 0mg; Calcium 17mg; Fibre 2.1g; Sodium 12mg.

Roast Mushroom Caps

Hunting for edible wild mushrooms is one of the Italians' great passions. The most prized are porcini, which grow in forests and are sometimes available fresh in the autumn in the UK.

Serves 4

4 large mushroom caps
2 garlic cloves, chopped
45ml/3 tbsp chopped
    fresh parsley

From the storecupboard
extra virgin olive oil, for drizzling
salt and ground black pepper

1 Preheat the oven to 190C°/375°F/Gas 5. Carefully wipe the mushrooms clean with a damp cloth or kitchen paper. Cut off the stems. (Save them for soup if they are not too woody). Oil a baking dish large enough to hold the mushrooms in one layer.

2 Place the mushroom caps in the dish, smooth side down. Mix together the chopped garlic and parsley and sprinkle the mixture over the mushroom caps.

3 Season the mushrooms with salt and pepper, then sprinkle with oil. Bake for 20–25 minutes until cooked through.

Aromatic Stewed Mushrooms

In this traditional recipe, from North-west Italy, the garlic is used to transform a simple dish of mushrooms into something that is quite memorable.

Serves 6

750g/1½lb fresh mushrooms, a
    mixture of wild and cultivated
2 garlic cloves, finely chopped
45m/3 tbsp chopped
    fresh parsley

From the storecupboard
90ml/6 tbsp olive oil
salt and ground black pepper

1 Clean the mushrooms carefully by wiping them with a damp cloth or kitchen paper.

2 Cut off the woody tips of the stems and discard. Slice the stems and caps fairly thickly.

3 Heat the oil in a large frying pan. Stir in the garlic and cook for about 1 minute. Add the mushrooms and cook for 8–10 minutes, stirring occasionally.

4 Season with salt and pepper and stir in the parsley. Cook for a further 5 minutes, then transfer to a warmed serving dish and serve immediately.

Slow-cooked Shiitake with Shoyu

Shiitake mushrooms cooked slowly are so rich and filling, that some people call them 'vegetarian steak'. This is a useful side dish which also makes a flavoursome addition to other dishes.

Serves 4

20 dried shiitake mushrooms
30ml/2 tbsp shoyu
5ml/1 tsp toasted sesame oil

From the storecupboard
30ml/2 tbsp vegetable oil

1 Start soaking the dried shiitake the day before. Put them in a large bowl almost full of water. Cover the shiitake with a plate or lid to stop them floating to the surface of the water. Leave to soak overnight.

2 Remove the shiitake from the soaking water and gently squeeze out the water with your fingers.

3 Measure 120ml/4fl oz/½ cup of the liquid in the bowl and set aside.

4 Heat the oil in a wok or a large frying pan. Stir-fry the shiitake over a high heat for 5 minutes, stirring continuously.

5 Reduce the heat to the lowest setting, then stir in the reserved soaking liquid and the shoyu.

6 Cook the mushrooms until there is almost no moisture left, stirring frequently. Sprinkle with the toasted sesame oil and remove from the heat.

7 Leave to cool, then slice and arrange the shiitake on a large plate and serve.

> **Cook's Tip**
> Ideally you should use a combination of both wild and cultivated mushrooms for this dish to give a nicely balanced flavour. A good mixture of mushroom varieties would be chanterelles and chestnut mushrooms: both are now sold in good supermarkets.

> **Variation**
> Cut the slow-cooked shiitake into thin strips. Mix with 600g/ 1⅓lb/5¼ cups cooked brown rice and 15ml/1 tbsp finely chopped chives. Sprinkle with toasted sesame seeds for a delicious rice.

Roast Mushroom Caps: Energy 104kcal/429kJ; Protein 3.2g; Carbohydrate 2.8g, of which sugars 0.7g; Fat 9g, of which saturates 1.3g; Cholesterol 0mg; Calcium 34mg; Fibre 2.2g; Sodium 10mg.
Stewed Mushrooms: Energy 122kcal/502kJ; Protein 2.7g; Carbohydrate 1.5g, of which sugars 0.5g; Fat 11.7g, of which saturates 1.7g; Cholesterol 0mg; Calcium 23mg; Fibre 1.9g; Sodium 9mg.
Shiitake with Shoyu: Energy 16kcal/69kJ; Protein 2g; Carbohydrate 1g, of which sugars 0.8g; Fat 0.5g, of which saturates 0.1g; Cholesterol 0mg; Calcium 7mg; Fibre 1.1g; Sodium 539mg.

Grilled Radicchio and Courgettes

Radicchio is often grilled or barbecued in Italian cooking to give it a special flavour. Combined with courgettes, it makes a quick and tasty side dish.

Serves 4
2–3 firm heads radicchio, round or long type, rinsed
4 courgettes (zucchini)

From the storecupboard
90ml/6 tbsp olive oil
salt and ground black pepper

1 Preheat the grill, cut the radicchio in half through the root section or base. Cut the courgettes into 1cm/½in diagonal slices.

2 When ready to cook, brush the vegetables with the olive oil and add salt and pepper. Cook for 4–5 minutes on each side.

Baked Courgettes with Cheese

This easy dish makes a great accompaniment to a wide range of main courses, or it can be served with some fresh crusty bread as a light lunch or supper dish for one or two. A piquant hard cheese, such as Desmond or Gabriel, made in West Cork, will give the courgettes character, or you could use a mature farmhouse Cheddar.

Serves 4
4 courgettes (zucchini)
30ml/2 tbsp grated hard farmhouse cheese, such as Gabriel or Desmond, or mature (sharp) farmhouse Cheddar

From the storecupboard
about 25g/1oz/2 tbsp butter
salt and ground black pepper

1 Preheat the oven to 180°C/350°F/Gas 4. Slice the courgettes in half, lengthways. Butter a shallow baking dish and arrange the courgettes, cut side up, inside the dish.

2 Sprinkle the cheese over the courgettes, and top with a few knobs (pats) of butter.

3 Bake in the preheated oven for about 20 minutes, or until the courgettes are tender and the cheese is bubbling and golden brown. Serve immediately.

Variation
The concentrated sweet flavour of sun-dried tomatoes complements courgettes (zucchini) well. Try the following dish which puts these two together in a colourful and mouthwatering way. Slice the 10 sun-dried tomatoes into thin strips. Place in a bowl with 175g/6fl oz/¾ cup warm water. Allow to stand for 20 minutes. Heat some oil in a large frying pan and stir in 1 large sliced onion. Cook gently to soften but do not allow to brown. Stir in 2 finely chopped garlic cloves and 1kg/2lb courgettes cut into thin strips. Cook for about 5 minutes, stirring. Stir in the tomatoes and their liquid. Season with salt and pepper. Increase the heat; cook until the courgettes are tender.

Marinated Courgettes

This is a simple low-fat vegetable dish that is prepared all over Italy using the best of the season's courgettes. It has a light and fresh flavour. It can be eaten hot or cold and is a delicious accompaniment to a main course.

Serves 6
4 courgettes (zucchini)
30ml/2 tbsp chopped fresh mint, plus whole leaves, to garnish
30ml/2 tbsp white wine vinegar

From the storecupboard
30ml/2 tbsp extra virgin olive oil
salt and ground black pepper

1 Cut the courgettes into thin slices using a sharp knife. Heat 15ml/1 tbsp of the oil in a large non-stick frying pan.

2 Fry the courgette slices in batches, for 4–6 minutes, or until tender and brown around the edges. Transfer to a bowl. Season.

3 Heat the remaining oil in the pan, then add the chopped mint and vinegar and let it bubble for a few seconds. Stir into the courgettes. Set aside to marinate for 1 hour, then serve garnished with mint leaves.

Courgettes with Cheese: Energy 96kcal/395kJ; Protein 3.8g; Carbohydrate 1.9g, of which sugars 1.8g; Fat 8g, of which saturates 5g; Cholesterol 21mg; Calcium 82mg; Fibre 0.9g; Sodium 93mg.
Radicchio and Courgettes: Energy 195kcal/802kJ; Protein 4.2g; Carbohydrate 4.9g, of which sugars 4.7g; Fat 17.7g, of which saturates 2.6g; Cholesterol 0mg; Calcium 71mg; Fibre 2.5g; Sodium 4mg.
Marinated Courgettes: Energy 60kcal/248kJ; Protein 2.7g; Carbohydrate 2.8g, of which sugars 2.3g; Fat 4.3g, of which saturates 0.7g; Cholesterol 0mg; Calcium 49mg; Fibre 1.2g; Sodium 3mg.

Caramelized Shallots

Sweet, golden shallots are good with all sorts of main dishes. Shallots have a less distinctive aroma than common onions and a milder flavour; they are also considered to be easier to digest. These caramelized shallots are also excellent with braised or roasted chestnuts, carrots or chunks of butternut squash. You may like to garnish the shallots with sprigs of fresh thyme before serving.

Serves 4–6
500g/1¼ lb shallots or small onions, peeled, with root ends intact
15ml/1 tbsp golden caster (superfine) sugar
30ml/2 tbsp red or white wine or port

From the storecupboard
50g/2oz/¼ cup butter or 60ml/4 tbsp olive oil
salt and ground black pepper

1 Heat the butter or oil in a large frying pan and add the shallots or onions in a single layer. Cook gently, turning occasionally, until they are lightly browned.

2 Sprinkle the sugar over the shallots and cook gently, turning the shallots in the juices, until the sugar begins to caramelize. Add the wine or port and let the mixture bubble for 4–5 minutes.

3 Add 150ml/¼ pint/⅔ cup water and seasoning. Cover and cook for 5 minutes, then remove the lid and cook until the liquid evaporates and the shallots are tender and glazed. Adjust the seasoning before serving.

Variation
A delicious alternative is shallots with chestnuts. Cook the shallots in butter or olive oil, then add 175ml/6fl oz/¾ cup water. Toss in 250–350g/9–12oz part-cooked chestnuts. Cook for 5–10 minutes, then serve, garnished with chopped flat leaf parsley.

Baked Onions

One of the oldest and most widely used flavouring vegetables, the onion, also deserves to be used more as a vegetable in its own right. Onions become sweet and mildly flavoured when slowly boiled or baked, and can be cooked very conveniently in the oven when baking potatoes or roasting parsnips. Not only do they make a tasty accompaniment to many dishes, but they also have a range of health benefits.

Serves 4
4 large even-sized onions

1 Preheat the oven to 180°C/350°F/Gas 4. Put a little cold water into a medium roasting pan, and arrange the unpeeled onions in it.

2 Bake in the preheated oven for about 1 hour, or until the onions feel soft when squeezed at the sides. Peel the skins and serve immediately.

Cook's Tip
These onions are baked in their skins, but you could peel them, if preferred, before baking. The peeled onions are best baked in a covered casserole dish instead of a roasting pan.

Variation
Sweet-sour roasted onions are a delicious variation on the onion theme. Cut 4 large onions into wedges, leaving them attached at the root end. Preheat the oven to 200°C/400°F/Gas 6. Put the onions in a roasting pan and pour over 60ml/4 tbsp olive oil. Sprinkle over 10ml/2 tsp crushed coriander seeds and mix thoroughly. Season, then roast for 20 minutes. Mix 15ml/1 tbsp honey with 30ml/2 tbsp pomegranate molasses, 15ml/1 tbsp sherry vinegar and 15ml/1 tbsp water. Drizzle over and stir. Reduce heat to 180°C/350°F/Gas 4 and cook for another 20–30 minutes.

Caramelized Shallots: Energy 96kcal/399kJ; Protein 1.3g; Carbohydrate 5.4g, of which sugars 5.4g; Fat 7.5g, of which saturates 1.1g; Cholesterol 0mg; Calcium 22mg; Fibre 1.2g; Sodium 9mg.
Baked Onions: Energy 90kcal/375kJ; Protein 3g; Carbohydrate 19.8g, of which sugars 14g; Fat 0.5g, of which saturates 0g; Cholesterol 0mg; Calcium 63mg; Fibre 3.5g; Sodium 8mg.

Leek Fritters

These crispy fried morsels are best served at room temperature, with a good squeeze of lemon juice and a sprinkling of salt and freshly grated nutmeg. Matzo meal, a traditional Jewish ingredient, is used in these fritters: it is made from crumbled matzo, an unleavened bread, similar to water biscuits. Matzo meal is used in a similar way to breadcrumbs, which can also be used to make these tasty fritters.

Serves 4

4 large leeks, total weight about 1kg/2¼lb, thickly sliced
120–175ml/4–6fl oz/½–¾ cup coarse matzo meal
2 eggs, lightly beaten

From the storecupboard
olive or vegetable oil, for shallow frying
salt and ground black pepper

1 Cook the leeks in salted boiling water for 5 minutes, or until just tender and bright green. Drain well and leave to cool.

2 Chop the leeks coarsely. Put in a bowl and combine with the matzo meal, eggs and seasoning.

3 Heat 5mm/¼in oil in a frying pan. Using two tablespoons, carefully spoon the leek mixture into the hot oil. Cook over a medium-high heat until golden brown on the underside, then turn and cook the second side.

4 Drain on kitchen paper. Add more oil if needed and heat before cooking more mixture.

> **Variation**
> *You can prepare other vegetables in the same way to wonderful effect. Try mushrooms, red (bell) pepper strips or carrots cut into thin batons, cooked briefly and combined, when cool, with either matzo meal or breadcrumbs and beaten egg, then lightly shallow fried.*

Cheesy Creamy Leeks

This is quite a rich accompaniment that could easily be served as a meal in itself with brown rice or couscous. Cheddar cheese has been used here for a slightly stronger flavour, but you could use a milder Swiss cheese, such as Gruyère, if you like.

Serves 4

4 large leeks or 12 baby leeks, trimmed and washed
150ml/¼ pint/⅔ cup double (heavy) cream
75g/3oz/¾ cup Cheddar or Monterey Jack cheese, grated

From the storecupboard
15ml/1 tbsp olive oil
salt and ground black pepper

1 Preheat the grill (broiler) to high. If using large leeks, slice them lengthways. Heat the oil in a large frying pan and add the leeks. Season with salt and pepper and cook for about 4 minutes, stirring occasionally, until starting to turn golden.

2 Pour the cream into the pan and stir until well combined. Allow to bubble gently for a few minutes.

3 Preheat the grill (broiler). Transfer the creamy leeks to a shallow ovenproof dish and sprinkle with the cheese. Grill (broil) for 4–5 minutes, or until the cheese is golden brown and bubbling and serve immediately.

> **Variation**
> *For a less rich alternative you could simply grill (broil) baby leeks. However, they will need blanching in boiling water for 2–3 minutes prior to grilling to soften the skins slightly. Once drained allow to cool a little, then gently squeeze out any excess water. Leave whole. Dry on a clean dish towel or on kitchen paper. Brush with oil, season with salt and pepper to taste, then grill, preferably in a griddle pan, for 3–4 minutes each side. The grilled leeks can be served hot, warm or cold. They are particularly delicious with a simple dressing of oil, vinegar, mustard and tarragon. Larger leeks can be used, but they will need a longer blanching and grilling time.*

Leek Fritters: Energy 227kcal/945kJ; Protein 5.8g; Carbohydrate 22.6g, of which sugars 2.7g; Fat 13.2g, of which saturates 1.8g; Cholesterol 48mg; Calcium 78mg; Fibre 3g; Sodium 18mg.
Cheesy Leeks: Energy 322kcal/1330kJ; Protein 7.8g; Carbohydrate 5g, of which sugars 4g; Fat 29.8g, of which saturates 17.1g; Cholesterol 70mg; Calcium 193mg; Fibre 3.3g; Sodium 147mg.

Roasted Jerusalem Artichokes

Jerusalem artichokes are in fact a member of the sunflower family. Now widely available, they conceal a deliciously sweet white flesh inside their knobbly brown exterior. While they are best known for soups, their natural sweetness enables them to glaze easily and they make a delicious side vegetable with many foods.

Serves 6
675g/1½lb Jerusalem artichokes
15ml/1 tbsp lemon juice
   or vinegar
seasoned flour, for dusting

From the storecupboard
50g/2oz/¼ cup unsalted
   (sweet) butter
salt

1 Peel the artichokes, dropping them straight into a bowl of water acidulated with lemon juice or vinegar to prevent browning. Cut up the artichokes so that the pieces are matched for size, otherwise they will cook unevenly.

2 Preheat the oven to 180°C/350°F/Gas 4. Bring a pan of salted water to the boil, drain the artichokes from the acidulated water and boil them for 5 minutes, or until just tender. Watch them carefully, as they have a tendency to break up easily.

3 Melt the butter in a roasting pan, coat the artichokes in the seasoned flour and roll them around in the butter in the pan.

4 Cook the butter and flour coated artichokes in the preheated oven for 20–30 minutes, or until golden brown. Serve immediately.

> **Variation**
> *Puréeing is a useful fall-back if the artichokes break up during cooking: simply blend or mash the drained boiled artichokes with salt and ground black pepper to taste and a little single (light) cream, if you like. Puréed artichokes are especially good served with game, which tends to be dry.*

Deep-fried Artichokes

The artichokes are baked, then pressed to open them and plunged into hot oil, where their leaves twist and brown, turning the artichokes into crispy flowers.

Serves 4
2–3 lemons, halved
4–8 small young globe artichokes

From the storecupboard
olive or vegetable oil, for
   deep-frying

1 Fill a large bowl with cold water and stir in the juice of one or two of the lemons. Trim and discard the stems of the artichokes, then trim off their tough ends and remove all the tough outer leaves until you reach the pale pointed centre. Carefully open the leaves of one of the artichokes by pressing it against the table or poking them open. Trim the tops if they are sharp.

2 If there is any choke inside the artichoke, remove it with a melon baller or small pointed spoon. Put in the acidulated water and prepare the remaining artichokes in the same way.

3 Put the artichokes in a large pan and pour over water to cover. Bring to the boil, reduce the heat and simmer for 10–15 minutes, or until partly cooked. If they are small, cook them for only 10 minutes. Drain the artichokes and leave upside down until cool enough to handle. Press them open gently, being careful not to break them apart.

4 Fill a pan with oil to a depth of 5–7.5cm/2–3in and heat. Add one or two artichokes at a time, with the leaves uppermost, and press down with a spoon to open up the leaves. Fry for 5–8 minutes, turning, until golden and crisp. Remove from the pan and drain on kitchen paper. Serve immediately, with the remaining lemon cut into wedges.

> **Cook's Tip**
> *Select immature artichokes, before their chokes have formed. Prepare and boil them ahead and deep-fry just before serving.*

Jerusalem Artichokes: Energy 101kcal/419kJ; Protein 0.7g; Carbohydrate 8.9g, of which sugars 8.4g; Fat 7.2g, of which saturates 4.5g; Cholesterol 18mg; Calcium 30mg; Fibre 2.7g; Sodium 242mg.
Deep-fried Artichokes: Energy 132kcal/546kJ; Protein 0.6g; Carbohydrate 1.1g, of which sugars 1.1g; Fat 14g, of which saturates 1.6g; Cholesterol 0mg; Calcium 51mg; Fibre 1.4g; Sodium 75mg.

Fennel, Potato and Garlic Mash

This flavoursome mash of potato, fennel and garlic goes well with practically any main course you can think of. Floury varieties of potato, such as Pentland Squire, King Edward or Marfona, are best for mashing as they produce a light, fluffy result. Waxy potatoes are more suitable for baking, or for salads, as they produce a dense, rather starchy mash.

Serves 4

800g/1¾ lb floury potatoes, cut into chunks
2 large fennel bulbs
120–150ml/4–5fl oz/½–⅔ cup milk or single (light) cream

From the storecupboard

90ml/6 tbsp garlic-flavoured olive oil
salt and ground black pepper

1 Boil the potatoes in water for 20 minutes, until tender.

2 Meanwhile, trim and chop the fennel, reserving any feathery tops. Chop the tops and set them aside.

3 Heat 30ml/2 tbsp of the oil in a pan. Add the fennel, cover and cook over a low heat for 20–30 minutes, until soft but not browned.

4 Drain and mash the potatoes. Purée the fennel in a food mill or blender and beat it into the potato with the remaining oil.

5 Warm the milk or cream and beat sufficient into the potato and fennel to make a creamy, light mixture. Season to taste and reheat gently, then beat in any chopped fennel tops. Serve immediately.

Cook's Tip
Cooking fennel tempers its aniseed flavour and brings out the delicious sweetness of the vegetable. Fennel is at its best when eaten fresh, so it should be kept in the refrigerator for a few days and eaten as soon as possible.

Spiced Asparagus Kale

Kale is a very important part of Scottish tradition. 'Kailyards' was the word used to describe the kitchen garden, and even the midday meal was often referred to as 'kail'. Use the more widely available curly kale if you find it hard to get the asparagus variety.

Serves 4

175g/6oz asparagus kale
10ml/2 tsp butter
25g/1 oz piece fresh root ginger, grated
15ml/1 tbsp soy sauce

From the storecupboard

salt and ground black pepper

1 Prepare the kale by removing the centre stalk and ripping the leaves into smallish pieces.

2 Heat a pan over a high heat and add the butter. As it melts, quickly add the kale and toss rapidly to allow the heat to cook it.

3 Grate the ginger into the pan and stir in thoroughly. Then add the soy sauce and mix well. When the kale has wilted, it is ready to serve.

Cook's Tip
Sea kale is a tasty variety which is commonly available between January and March. Its pale green fronds have a slightly nutty taste. It doesn't need cooking but should be washed and drained thoroughly before eating.

Variation
Kale with mustard dressing is traditionally made with sea kale, but any kale or dark green cabbage can be substituted. If using alternatives, boil the leaves for a few minutes before chilling. Whisk 45ml/3 tbsp of olive oil into 5ml/1 tsp wholegrain mustard. Next, whisk in 15ml/1 tbsp white wine vinegar. When it thickens, season with a pinch of caster sugar, salt and ground black pepper. Toss the kale in the dressing and serve at once.

Fennel/Potato Mash: Energy 144kcal/608kJ; Protein 4g; Carbohydrate 24.4g, of which sugars 4.6g; Fat 4.1g, of which saturates 2.3g; Cholesterol 10mg; Calcium 60mg; Fibre 4g; Sodium 61mg.
Spiced Asparagus Kale: Energy 35kcal/145kJ; Protein 1.6g; Carbohydrate 0.9g, of which sugars 0.9g; Fat 2.8g, of which saturates 1.4g; Cholesterol 5mg; Calcium 58mg; Fibre 1.4g; Sodium 301mg.

Green Beans Tempura

This crispy Japanese dish is distinguished by the green beans, which are coated in a light tempura batter.

Serves 4
400g/14oz green beans
100g/3¾oz/scant 1 cup plain (all-purpose) flour
1 egg

From the storecupboard
vegetable oil, for deep-frying
salt

1 Trim the beans and blanch in a large pan of boiling water for 1 minute. Drain and refresh in iced water, then drain again well.

2 Sift the flour into a bowl and stir in enough cold water to make a paste. Add the egg and beat well, then season with salt.

3 Heat the oil in a large pan or deep-fryer to 170°C/340°F. Dip the beans in the batter, add to the hot oil and deep-fry until golden brown. Drain on kitchen paper and serve.

Green Beans with Almond Butter

A perfect accompaniment for all manner of mains.

Serves 4
350g/12oz green beans, trimmed
50g/2oz/⅓ cup whole blanched almonds

grated rind and juice of 1 unwaxed lemon

From the storecupboard
50g/2oz/¼ cup butter
salt and ground black pepper

1 Cook the beans in a pan of salted, boiling water for about 3 minutes, or until just tender. Drain well. Meanwhile, melt the butter in a large non-stick pan until foamy.

2 Add the almonds to the pan and cook, stirring occasionally, for 2–3 minutes, or until golden. Remove from the heat and toss with the beans, lemon rind and juice. Season.

Cauliflower with Garlic Crumbs

This simple dish makes a great accompaniment to main dishes. When buying cauliflower look for creamy white coloured florets with the inner green leaves curled round the flower. Discard cauliflowers with discoloured patches or yellow leaves. As an alternative, try using broccoli florets instead of the cauliflower. Broccoli should have a fresh appearance: avoid yellowing specimens and those that feel soft or are wilting.

Serves 4–6
1 large cauliflower, cut into bitesize florets
130g/4½oz/2¼ cups dry white or wholemeal (whole-wheat) breadcrumbs
3–5 garlic cloves, thinly sliced or chopped

From the storecupboard
90–120ml/6–8 tbsp olive or vegetable oil
salt and ground black pepper

1 Steam or boil the cauliflower in salted water until just tender. Drain and leave to cool.

2 Heat 60–75ml/4–5 tbsp of the olive or vegetable oil in a pan, add the breadcrumbs and cook over a medium heat, tossing and turning, until browned and crisp. Add the garlic, turn once or twice, then remove from the pan and set aside.

3 Heat the remaining oil in the pan, then add the cauliflower, mashing and breaking it up a little as it lightly browns in the oil. (Do not overcook but just cook until lightly browned.)

4 Add the garlic breadcrumbs to the pan and cook, stirring, until well combined, with some of the cauliflower still holding its shape. Season and serve hot or warm.

Cook's Tip
Serve this garlicky cauliflower dish as they do in Italy, with cooked pasta, such as spaghetti.

Beans Tempura: Energy 227kcal/945kJ; Protein 5.8g; Carbohydrate 22.6g, of which sugars 2.7g; Fat 13.2g, of which saturates 1.8g; Cholesterol 48mg; Calcium 78mg; Fibre 3g; Sodium 18mg.
Green Beans: Energy 191kcal/786kJ; Protein 4.4g; Carbohydrate 3.7g, of which sugars 2.6g; Fat 17.7g, of which saturates 7.2g; Cholesterol 27mg; Calcium 64mg; Fibre 2.9g; Sodium 78mg.
Cauliflower: Energy 244kcal/1016kJ; Protein 8.9g; Carbohydrate 18.8g, of which sugars 2.2g; Fat 15.3g, of which saturates 3.8g; Cholesterol 10mg; Calcium 162mg; Fibre 1.7g; Sodium 280mg.

Gingered Carrots

Broccoli with Oil and Garlic

This is a very simple way of transforming steamed or blanched broccoli into a succulent Mediterranean dish. Peeling the broccoli stalks is easy and allows for even cooking.

Serves 6
1kg/2lb fresh broccoli
2–3 garlic cloves, finely chopped

From the storecupboard
90ml/6 tbsp olive oil
salt and ground black pepper

1 Wash the broccoli. Cut off any woody parts at the base of the stems. Using a small sharp knife, peel the broccoli stems. Cut any very long or wide stalks in half.

2 If steaming the broccoli, place water in the bottom of a pan equipped with a steamer and bring to the boil. Put the broccoli in the steamer, cover tightly and cook for 8–12 minutes, or until the stems are just tender when pierced with the point of a knife. Remove from the heat.

3 If blanching the broccoli, bring a large pan of water to the boil, drop the broccoli into the pan of boiling water and blanch for 5–6 minutes, until just tender. Drain.

4 In a frying pan large enough to hold all the broccoli pieces, gently heat the oil with the garlic.

5 When the garlic is light golden (do not let it brown or it will be bitter) add the broccoli and cook over medium heat for 3–4 minutes, turning carefully to coat it with the hot oil. Season with salt and pepper. Serve hot or cold.

This fresh and zesty salad is ideal served as an accompaniment to many main courses. Some food processors have an attachment that can be used to cut the carrots into batons, which makes quick work of the preparation, but even cutting them by hand doesn't take too long. Fresh root ginger goes perfectly with sweet carrots, and the tiny black poppy seeds not only add taste and texture, but also look stunning against the bright orange of the carrots.

Serves 4
350g/12oz carrots, peeled and
    cut into fine matchsticks
2.5cm/1in piece of fresh root
    ginger, peeled and grated
15ml/1 tbsp poppy seeds

From the storecupboard
30ml/2 tbsp garlic-infused olive oil
salt and ground black pepper

1 Put the carrots in a bowl and stir in the oil and grated ginger. Cover and chill for a minium of 30 minutes, to allow the flavours to develop.

2 Season the salad with salt and pepper to taste. Stir in the poppy seeds just before serving.

Variation
To make a parsnip and sesame seed salad, replace the carrots with parsnips and blanch in boiling salted water for 1 minute before combining with the oil and ginger. Replace the poppy seeds with the same quantity of sesame seeds.

Cook's Tip
The sweetness of carrots can be heightened by adding Marsala wine and sugar – a traditional Sicilian dish. Cut carrots into sticks, melt butter, add sugar and salt, then stir in a small amount of Marsala. Just cover with water and cook until tender with a lid on. Uncover and reduce the liquid down.

Variation
To turn the dish into a topping for pasta, add about 25g/1oz each fresh breadcrumbs and pine nuts to the garlic at the beginning of step 4 and cook until golden. Then add the broccoli with 25g/1oz sultanas (golden raisins) and some chopped fresh parsley. Toss into cooked pasta and serve with roasted tomatoes.

Gingered Carrot Salad: Energy 103kcal/424kJ; Protein 1.2g; Carbohydrate 7g, of which sugars 6.5g; Fat 7.9g, of which saturates 1.2g; Cholesterol 0mg; Calcium 47mg; Fibre 2.4g; Sodium 23mg.
Broccoli with Garlic: Energy 159kcal/657kJ; Protein 7.7g; Carbohydrate 3.8g, of which sugars 2.6g; Fat 12.5g, of which saturates 1.9g; Cholesterol 0mg; Calcium 94mg; Fibre 4.5g; Sodium 14mg.

Broccoli with Soy Sauce

A wonderfully simple dish that you will want to make again and again. The broccoli cooks in next to no time, so don't start cooking until you are almost ready to eat.

Serves 4
450g/1lb broccoli
2 garlic cloves, crushed
30ml/2 tbsp light soy sauce
fried garlic slices, to garnish

From the storecupboard
15ml/1 tbsp vegetable oil
salt

1 Cut the thick stems from the broccoli; cut off any particularly woody bits, then cut the stems lengthways into thin slices. Separate the head of the broccoli into large florets.

2 Bring a pan of lightly salted water to the boil. Add the broccoli and cook for 3–4 minutes until tender but still crisp.

3 Transfer the broccoli to a colander, drain thoroughly and arrange in a heated serving dish.

4 Heat the oil in a small pan. Fry the garlic for 2 minutes to release the flavour, then remove it with a slotted spoon. Pour the oil carefully over the broccoli, taking care as it will splatter. Drizzle the soy sauce over the broccoli, sprinkle over the fried garlic and serve.

> **Cook's Tip**
> Fried garlic slices make a good garnish but take care that the oil used does not get too hot; if the garlic burns, it will taste unpleasantly bitter.

> **Variation**
> Most leafy vegetables taste delicious prepared this way. Try blanched cos or romaine lettuce and you may be surprised at how crisp and clean the taste is.

Stir-fried Broccoli with Soy Sauce and Sesame Seeds

Purple sprouting broccoli has been used for this recipe, but when it is not available an alternative variety of broccoli, such as calabrese, will also work very well.

Serves 2
225g/8oz purple sprouting broccoli
15ml/1 tbsp soy sauce
15ml/1 tbsp toasted sesame seeds

From the storecupboard
15ml/1 tbsp olive oil
salt and ground black pepper

1 Using a sharp knife, cut off and discard any thick stems from the broccoli and cut the broccoli into long, thin florets.

2 Heat the olive oil in a wok or large frying pan and add the broccoli. Stir-fry for 3–4 minutes, or until tender, adding a splash of water if the pan becomes too dry.

3 Add the soy sauce to the broccoli, then season with salt and ground black pepper to taste. Add sesame seeds, toss to combine and serve immediately.

> **Cook's Tip**
> Other vegetables from the brassica family could be substituted for broccoli, such as cauliflower, which can be prepared in the same way. Alternatively, try some shredded cabbage, pak choi (bok choy) or Brussels sprouts.

> **Variation**
> An essential part of the Asian diet for centuries, seaweed is now acknowledged in other parts of the world for its amazing health benefits. Try making this recipe with shredded nori, laver or arame.

Broccoli with Soy Sauce: Energy 65kcal/271kJ; Protein 5.2g; Carbohydrate 2.7g, of which sugars 2.2g; Fat 3.8g, of which saturates 0.6g; Cholesterol 0mg; Calcium 64mg; Fibre 2.9g; Sodium 543mg.
Broccoli and Sesame: Energy 135kcal/558kJ; Protein 6.6g; Carbohydrate 2.7g, of which sugars 2.3g; Fat 10.9g, of which saturates 1.7g; Cholesterol 0mg; Calcium 115mg; Fibre 3.5g; Sodium 545mg.

Summer Squash and Baby New Potatoes in Warm Dill Sour Cream

Fresh vegetables and fragrant dill are delicious tossed in a simple sour cream or yogurt sauce. Choose small squash with bright skins that are free from blemishes and bruises. To make a simpler potato salad, pour the dill sour cream over warm cooked new potatoes.

Serves 4
400g/14oz mixed squash, such as
    yellow and green courgettes
    (zucchini), and green patty pan
400g/14oz baby new potatoes
1 large handful mixed fresh dill
    and chives, finely chopped
300ml/½ pint/1¼ cups sour
    cream or Greek (US strained
    plain) yogurt

From the storecupboard
salt and ground black pepper

1 Cut the squash into pieces about the same size as the potatoes. Put the potatoes in a pan and add water to cover and a pinch of salt. Bring to the boil, then simmer for about 10 minutes, until almost tender. Add the squash and continue to cook until the vegetables are just tender, then drain.

2 Put the vegetables into a wide, shallow pan and gently stir in the finely chopped fresh dill and chives.

3 Remove the pan from the heat and stir in the sour cream or yogurt. Return to the heat and heat gently until warm. Season and serve.

> **Cook's Tip**
> *Summer squash are picked when still young and the skins are tender and edible. Included in this group are patty pan, courgettes (zucchini), marrows and cucumber. Summer squash do not keep well, so should only be stored in the refrigerator for a few days, unlike winter squash, which can be kept for several weeks in a cool dark place.*

Baked Winter Squash with Tomatoes

Acorn, butternut or Hubbard squash can all be used in this simple recipe. Serve the squash as a side dish or as a light main course, with warm crusty bread. Canned chopped tomatoes with herbs are used in this recipe. A wide variety of flavoured canned tomatoes are now available, including some with garlic, onion and olives – they are ideal for adding a combination of flavours when time is short.

Serves 4–6
1kg/2¼lb pumpkin or orange
    winter squash, peeled
    and sliced
2 x 400g/14oz cans chopped
    tomatoes with herbs
2–3 rosemary sprigs, stems
    removed and leaves chopped

From the storecupboard
45ml/3 tbsp garlic-flavoured
    olive oil
salt and ground black pepper

1 Preheat the oven to 160°C/325°F/Gas 3. Heat the oil in a pan and cook the pumpkin or squash slices, in batches, until golden brown, removing them from the pan as soon as they are cooked.

2 Add the tomatoes and cook over a medium-high heat until the mixture is of a sauce consistency. Stir in the rosemary and season to taste with salt and pepper.

3 Layer the pumpkin slices and tomatoes alternately in an ovenproof dish, finishing with a layer of tomatoes. Bake for 35 minutes, or until the top layer is lightly glazed and is beginning to turn golden brown, and the pumpkin is tender. Serve immediately.

> **Cook's Tip**
> *This dish can be blended in a food processor to make a tasty purée, fantastic with rice or couscous, or transformed into a soup with a little added stock or milk for a more subtle, creamier result.*

Baked Winter Squash: Energy 94kcal/392kJ; Protein 2.1g; Carbohydrate 7.8g, of which sugars 7g; Fat 6.2g, of which saturates 1.1g; Cholesterol 0mg; Calcium 58mg; Fibre 3g; Sodium 12mg.
Summer Squash: Energy 317kcal/1317kJ; Protein 5.8g; Carbohydrate 21g, of which sugars 6.1g; Fat 23.9g, of which saturates 14.8g; Cholesterol 66mg; Calcium 105mg; Fibre 2g; Sodium 104mg.

Spicy Potato Wedges

Serve on their own with a dip or as an accompaniment to a main dish.

Serves 4

675g/1½lb floury potatoes, such as Maris Piper

10ml/2 tsp paprika
5ml/1 tsp ground cumin

From the storecupboard
45ml/3 tbsp olive oil
salt and ground black pepper

1 Preheat the oven to 190°C/375°F/Gas 5. Using a sharp knife, cut the potatoes into chunky wedges and put in a roasting pan.

2 In a small bowl, combine the olive oil with the paprika and cumin and season well. Pour the mixture over the potatoes and toss well to coat thoroughly. Spread the potatoes out in the roasting pan and bake for 30–40 minutes, or until golden brown. Serve immediately.

Garlicky Roasties

Potatoes roasted in their skins retain a deep, earthy taste (and absorb less fat) while the garlic mellows on cooking to give a pungent but not overly-strong taste to serve alongside or squeezed over as a garnish.

Serves 4

1kg/2¼lb small floury potatoes
10ml/2 tsp walnut oil
2 whole garlic bulbs, unpeeled

From the storecupboard
60–75ml/4–5 tbsp sunflower oil
salt and ground black pepper

1 Preheat the oven to 240°C/475°F/Gas 9. Place the potatoes in a pan of cold water and bring to the boil. Drain.

2 Combine the oils in a roasting tin and place in the oven to get really hot. Add the potatoes and garlic and coat in oil.

3 Sprinkle with salt and roast for 10 minutes. Reduce the heat to 200°C/400°F/Gas 6. Continue roasting, basting occasionally, for 30–40 minutes. Serve each portion with some garlic cloves.

Crisp and Golden Roast Potatoes

These golden roast potatoes are wonderfully crispy and have a fantastic flavour. If you like, add a couple of bay leaves to the potatoes before roasting; they impart a lovely flavour.

Serves 4

675g/1½lb floury potatoes, such as Maris Piper, peeled
15ml/1 tbsp olive oil or large knob of butter
12 garlic cloves, unpeeled

From the storecupboard
salt and ground black pepper

1 Preheat the oven to 190°C/375°F/Gas 5. Cut the potatoes into large chunks and cook in a pan of salted, boiling water for 5 minutes. Drain well and give the colander a good shake to fluff up the edges of the potatoes.

2 Return the potatoes to the pan and place it over a low heat for 1 minute to steam off any excess water.

3 Meanwhile, spoon the olive oil or butter into a roasting pan and place in the oven until hot, about 5 minutes.

4 Add the potatoes to the pan with the garlic and turn to coat in the oil or butter.

5 Season well with salt and ground black pepper and roast for 40–50 minutes, turning occasionally, until the potatoes are golden and tender.

Variation
For a more substantial dish, try roasting diced butternut squash and baby carrots with the potatoes.

Cook's Tip
Tasty roast potatoes are high in calories so should be reserved as a treat to cook on special occasions.

Spicy Wedges: Energy 200kcal/838kJ; Protein 3.3g; Carbohydrate 28.1g, of which sugars 2.2g; Fat 9.1g, of which saturates 1.4g; Cholesterol 0mg; Calcium 15mg; Fibre 1.7g; Sodium 20mg.
Garlicky Roasties: Energy 312kcal/1310kJ; Protein 6.2g; Carbohydrate 44.3g, of which sugars 3.7g; Fat 13.4g, of which saturates 1.7g; Cholesterol 0mg; Calcium 20mg; Fibre 3.5g; Sodium 29mg.
Crisp Roast Potatoes: Energy 185kcal/778kJ; Protein 2.9g; Carbohydrate 27.2g, of which sugars 2.2g; Fat 7.9g, of which saturates 3.2g; Cholesterol 7mg; Calcium 10mg; Fibre 1.7g; Sodium 19mg.

Grilled Corn on the Cob

Keeping the husks on the corn protects the corn kernels and encloses the butter, so the flavours are contained. Fresh corn with husks intact are perfect, but banana leaves or a double layer of foil are also suitable to wrap corn for cooking corn on the barbecue.

Serves 6
3 dried chipotle chillies
7.5ml/1½ tsp lemon juice
45ml/3 tbsp chopped fresh flat
    leaf parsley
6 corn on the cob, with
    husks intact

From the storecupboard
250g/9oz/generous 1 cup
    butter softened
salt and ground black pepper

1 Heat a frying pan. Add the dried chillies and roast them by stirring them for 1 minute without letting them scorch. Put them in a bowl with almost boiling water to cover. Use a saucer to keep them submerged, and leave them to rehydrate for up to 1 hour.

2 Drain, remove the seeds and chop the chillies finely. Place the butter in a bowl and add the chillies, lemon juice and parsley. Season to taste and mix well.

3 Peel back the husks from each cob without tearing them. Remove the silk. Smear about 30ml/2 tbsp of the chilli butter over each cob. Pull the husks back over the cobs, ensuring that the butter is well hidden.

4 Put the rest of the butter in a pot, smooth the top and chill to use later. Place the cobs in a bowl of cold water and leave in a cool place for 1–3 hours or longer if it suits you better.

5 Prepare the barbecue. Remove the corn cobs from the water and wrap in pairs in foil. Once the flames have died down, position a lightly oiled grill rack over the coals to heat. When the coals are medium-hot, or have a moderate coating of ash, grill the corn for 15–20 minutes. Remove the foil and cook them for about 5 minutes more, turning them often to char the husks a little. Serve hot, with the rest of the butter.

Hot Avocado Halves

If you make the basil oil in advance, or buy a ready prepared basil oil, this is an ultra-simple dish. It makes an eye-catching side dish and is also an excellent appetite teaser to serve while the rest of the food is on the barbecue.

Serves 6
3 ready-to-eat avocados,
    preferably Hass for flavour
105ml/7 tbsp balsamic vinegar

For the basil oil
40g/1½ oz/1½ cups fresh basil
    leaves, stalks removed
200ml/7fl oz/scant 1 cup olive oil

1 To make the basil oil, place the leaves in a bowl and pour boiling water over. Leave for 30 seconds. Drain, refresh under cold water and drain again. Squeeze dry and pat with kitchen paper to remove as much moisture as possible.

2 Place in a food processor with the oil and process to a purée. Put into a bowl, cover and chill overnight.

3 Next day, line a sieve (strainer) with muslin (cheesecloth), set it over a deep bowl and pour in the basil purée. Leave undisturbed for 1 hour, or until all the oil has filtered into the bowl. Discard the solids and pour into a bottle, then chill until ready to cook.

4 Prepare the barbecue. Cut each avocado in half and prise out the stone (pit). Brush with a little of the basil oil.

5 Heat the balsamic vinegar gently in a pan, on the stove or on the barbecue. When it starts to boil, simmer for 1 minute, or until it is just beginning to turn slightly syrupy.

6 Heat the griddle on the grill rack over hot coals. (Remember it is ready to use when a few drops of water sprinkled on the surface evaporate instantly.) Lower the heat a little and place the avocado halves cut side down on the griddle.

7 Cook for 30–60 seconds, until branded with grill marks. (Move the avocados around carefully with tongs to create a chequered effect.) Serve hot with the vinegar and extra oil.

Hot Avocado Halves: Energy 222kcal/916kJ; Protein 1g; Carbohydrate 1g, of which sugars 0.3g; Fat 23.8g, of which saturates 4.1g; Cholesterol 0mg; Calcium 6mg; Fibre 1.7g; Sodium 3mg.
Grilled Corn: Energy 435kcal/1805kJ; Protein 3.4g; Carbohydrate 27.1g, of which sugars 10g; Fat 35.6g, of which saturates 21.9g; Cholesterol 89mg; Calcium 28mg; Fibre 1.8g; Sodium 525mg.

Butter Bean, Tomato and Red Onion Salad

Serve this salad with toasted pitta bread for a fresh summer lunch, or as an accompaniment to a main course.

Serves 4
2 x 400g/14oz cans butter (lima) beans, rinsed and drained
4 plum tomatoes, roughly chopped
1 red onion, finely sliced

From the storecupboard
45ml/3 tbsp herb-infused olive oil
salt and ground black pepper

1 Mix together the beans, tomatoes and onion in a large bowl. Season with salt and pepper, and stir in the oil.

2 Cover the bowl with clear film (plastic wrap) and chill for 20 minutes before serving.

Variations
• *To add a bit of extra flavour and colour, try stirring in a handful of pitted black olives and a handful of chopped fresh parsley.*
• *To make a wholesome version of the Italian salad panzanella, tear half a loaf of ciabatta into bitesize pieces and stir into the salad. Leave to stand for 20 minutes before serving.*

Potato, Caraway Seed and Parsley Salad

Leaving the potatoes to cool in garlic-infused oil with the caraway seeds helps them to absorb plenty of flavour.

15ml/1 tbsp caraway seeds, lightly crushed
45ml/3 tbsp chopped fresh parsley

Serves 4–6
675g/1½ lb new potatoes, scrubbed

From the storecupboard
45ml/3 tbsp garlic-infused olive oil
salt and ground black pepper

1 Cook the potatoes in salted, boiling water for about 10 minutes, or until just tender. Drain thoroughly and transfer to a large bowl.

2 Stir the oil, caraway seeds and some salt and pepper into the hot potatoes, then set aside to cool. When the potatoes are almost cold, stir in the parsley and serve.

Variation
This recipe is also delicious made with sweet potatoes instead of new potatoes. Peel and roughly chop the sweet potatoes, then follow the recipe as before.

Aubergines with Feta and Coriander

Aubergines take on a lovely smoky flavour when grilled on a barbecue, which contrasts beautifully with the sharpness of the feta cheese. Choose a good quality Greek feta cheese for the best flavour.

Serves 6
3 medium aubergines (eggplants)
400g/14oz feta cheese
a small bunch of coriander (cilantro), roughly chopped

From the storecupboard
60ml/4 tbsp extra virgin olive oil
salt and ground black pepper

1 Prepare a barbecue. Cook the aubergines for 20 minutes, turning occasionally, until charred and soft. Remove from the barbecue and cut in half lengthways.

2 Carefully scoop the aubergine flesh into a bowl, reserving the skins. Mash the flesh roughly with a fork.

3 Crumble the feta cheese, then stir into the mashed aubergine with the chopped coriander and olive oil. Season with salt and ground black pepper to taste.

4 Spoon the aubergine and feta mixture back into the skins and return to the barbecue for 5 minutes to warm through. Serve immediately.

Cook's Tip
When buying aubergines, look for small- to medium-sized vegetables, which have sweet tender flesh. They can be stored in the refrigerator for up to two weeks.

Variation
Other chopped fresh herbs are equally good in this dish. Why not try mint or basil, or flat leaf parsley? Serve with some sliced ripe beef tomatoes drizzled with olive oil for a delicious alfresco lunch.

Butter Bean and Tomato: Energy 156kcal/658kJ; Protein 8.7g; Carbohydrate 21.4g, of which sugars 4.9g; Fat 4.6g, of which saturates 0.7g; Cholesterol 0mg; Calcium 31mg; Fibre 7.2g; Sodium 567mg.
Potato, Caraway and Parsley: Energy 131kcal/549kJ; Protein 2.1g; Carbohydrate 18.3g, of which sugars 1.6g; Fat 5.9g, of which saturates 0.9g; Cholesterol 0mg; Calcium 22mg; Fibre 1.5g; Sodium 15mg.
Aubergines with Feta: Energy 257kcal/1066kJ; Protein 12g; Carbohydrate 4.2g, of which sugars 3.9g; Fat 21.5g, of which saturates 10.3g; Cholesterol 47mg; Calcium 286mg; Fibre 3.3g; Sodium 968mg.

Okra with Tomatoes and Coriander

This is a favourite Middle Eastern way to prepare okra. Add wedges of lemon as a garnish so that their juice can be squeezed over the vegetables to taste. Okra, also known as lady's fingers, are narrow green lantern-shaped pods. They contain a row of seeds that ooze a viscous liquid when cooked. This liquid acts as a natural thickener in a variety of curries and soups.

Serves 4–6

400g/14oz can chopped
   tomatoes with onions and garlic
generous pinch each of ground
   cinnamon, cumin and cloves
90ml/6 tbsp chopped fresh
   coriander (cilantro) leaves
800g/1¾lb okra

From the storecupboard
salt and ground black pepper

1 Heat the tomatoes and the cinnamon, cumin and cloves with half the coriander in a pan, then season to taste with salt and ground black pepper and bring to the boil.

2 Add the okra and cook, stirring constantly, for 1–2 minutes. Reduce the heat to low, then simmer, stirring occasionally, for 20–30 minutes, until the okra is tender.

3 Taste for spicing and seasoning, and adjust if necessary, adding more of any one spice, salt or pepper to taste. Stir in the remaining coriander. Serve hot, warm or cold.

> **Cook's Tip**
> Fresh okra is widely available from most supermarkets and Asian stores. Choose firm, green specimens and avoid any that are limp or turning brown.

> **Variation**
> Okra can be stir-fried with chilli and spices, then sprinkled with freshly grated coconut for an exotic twist.

Creamy Polenta with Dolcelatte

Soft-cooked polenta, which is made from cornmeal, is a tasty accompaniment to main dishes and makes a delicious change from the usual potatoes or rice. It can also be enjoyed on its own as a hearty snack.

Serves 4–6

900ml/1½ pints/3¾ cups milk
115g/4oz/1 cup instant polenta
115g/4oz Dolcelatte cheese

From the storecupboard
60ml/4 tbsp extra virgin olive oil
salt and ground black pepper

1 Pour the milk into a large pan and bring to the boil, then add a good pinch of salt. Remove the pan from the heat and pour in the polenta in a slow, steady stream, stirring constantly to combine.

2 Return the pan to a low heat and simmer gently, stirring constantly, for 5 minutes. Remove the pan from the heat and stir in the olive oil.

3 Spoon the polenta into a serving dish and crumble the cheese over the top. Season with more ground black pepper and serve immediately.

> **Variation**
> In place of Dolcelatte cheese, you can stir in the same quantity of grated mature (sharp) Cheddar or freshly grated Parmesan. To this you can add a handful of chopped fresh herbs, such as sage, oregano or thyme.

> **Cook's Tip**
> There are a variety of ways to serve polenta besides the soft cooked method, such as grilling (broiling) and frying. Pour the cooked polenta into an oiled tray to about 1cm/½in thick, allow to set and then chill for 20 minutes. Turn out on to a chopping board and cut into squares or triangles, then grill or fry until golden brown and add the topping of your choice.

Okra with Tomatoes: Energy 56kcal/234kJ; Protein 4.5g; Carbohydrate 6.3g, of which sugars 5.6g; Fat 1.6g, of which saturates 0.5g; Cholesterol 0mg; Calcium 235mg; Fibre 6.4g; Sodium 20mg.
Creamy Polenta: Energy 271kcal/1131kJ; Protein 10.8g; Carbohydrate 21.1g, of which sugars 7.1g; Fat 16.1g, of which saturates 6.3g; Cholesterol 23mg; Calcium 274mg; Fibre 0.4g; Sodium 298mg.

Soft Fried Noodles

This is a great dish for times when you are feeling a little peckish and fancy something simple but satisfying. Drain the cooked noodles and ladle them into the wok a few at a time, swirling them with the onions, so they don't all clump together on contact with the hot oil.

Serves 4–6

6–8 spring onions (scallions)
350g/12oz dried egg noodles,
    cooked and drained
soy sauce and chopped coriander
    (cilantro), to taste

From the storecupboard

30ml/2 tbsp vegetable oil
salt and ground black pepper

1 Heat the oil in a wok. Shred the spring onions and fry for about 30 seconds. Add the noodles and separate the strands. Fry the noodles until they are heated through, lightly browned and crisp on the outside, but still soft inside. Season with soy sauce, chopped coriander, and salt and pepper. Serve immediately.

Bocconcini with Fennel and Basil

These tiny balls of mozzarella are best when they're perfectly fresh. They should be milky and soft when you cut into them. Buy them from an Italian delicatessen or a good cheese shop. If you can't get hold of them, cut a ball of mozzarella into bitesizes.

Serves 6

450g/1lb bocconcini mozzarella
5ml/1 tsp fennel seeds,
    lightly crushed
a small bunch of fresh basil
    leaves, roughly torn

From the storecupboard

45ml/3 tbsp extra virgin olive oil
salt and ground black pepper

1 Drain the bocconcini well and place in a bowl. Stir in the olive oil, fennel seeds and basil, and season with salt and pepper. Cover and chill for 1 hour.

2 Remove the bowl from the refrigerator and leave to stand for about 30 minutes for the cheese to return to room temperature before serving.

Noodles with Sesame Spring Onions

You can use any kind of noodles for this Asian-style dish. Rice noodles look and taste particularly good, but egg noodles work just as well. This dish can be served hot, or chilled as a salad.

Serves 4

1 bunch of spring onions
    (scallions), trimmed
225g/8oz flat rice noodles
30ml/2 tbsp soy sauce

From the storecupboard

30ml/2 tbsp sesame oil
salt and ground black pepper

1 Preheat the oven to 200°C/400°F/Gas 6. Cut the spring onions into three pieces, then put them in a small roasting pan and season with salt and pepper.

2 Drizzle the sesame oil over the spring onions and roast for 10 minutes, until they are slightly charred and tender. Set aside.

3 Cook the noodles according to the instructions on the packet and drain thoroughly. Toss with the spring onions and oyster sauce, and season with ground black pepper. Serve immediately.

> **Cook's Tips**
> These noodles taste even better when served with a sprinkling of toasted sesame seeds.

> **Variation**
> Spicy peanut noodles are a tasty alternative side dish. Cook a 250g/9oz packet of egg noodles according to the instructions. Drain. Then heat 15ml/1 tbsp sunflower oil in a wok and add 30ml/2 tbsp crunchy peanut butter. Add a splash of cold water and a dash of soy sauce and stir the mixture over a gentle heat until thoroughly combined. Add the noodles to the pan and toss to coat in the peanut mixture. Sprinkle with fresh coriander (cilantro) to serve.

Soft Fried Noodles: Energy 262kcal/1107kJ; Protein 7.2g; Carbohydrate 42g, of which sugars 1.3g; Fat 8.5g, of which saturates 1.8g; Cholesterol 18mg; Calcium 18mg; Fibre 1.8g; Sodium 105mg.
Bocconcini: Energy 245kcal/1015kJ; Protein 14.2g; Carbohydrate 0.2g, of which sugars 0.2g; Fat 20.8g, of which saturates 11.1g; Cholesterol 44mg; Calcium 288mg; Fibre 0.4g; Sodium 299mg.
Noodles with Sesame: Energy 266kcal/1111kJ; Protein 3.4g; Carbohydrate 48.8g, of which sugars 2.8g; Fat 5.7g, of which saturates 0.8g; Cholesterol 0mg; Calcium 18mg; Fibre 0.5g; Sodium 131mg.

Corn Tortillas

These delicious and versatile Mexican specialities cook very quickly. Griddle them over the barbecue and have a clean dish towel on hand to keep the hot stacks warm.

Makes about 14
275g/10oz/2½ cups masa harina

1 Prepare the barbecue. Put the masa harina into a bowl and stir in 250ml/8fl oz/1 cup of water, mixing it to a soft dough that just holds together. If it is too dry, add a little more water. Cover the bowl with a cloth and set aside for 15 minutes.

2 Knead the dough lightly then divide into 14 pieces, and shape into balls.

3 Using a rolling pin, roll out each ball between sheets of clear film (plastic wrap) until you have a thin round of dough measuring about 15cm/6in in diameter.

4 Put a griddle over the hot coals and griddle the first tortilla for 1 minute. Turn it over and cook for a minute more. Wrap in a clean dish towel and keep warm. Repeat for the other tortillas.

> **Cook's Tips**
> • *When making tortillas, it is important to get the dough texture right. If it is too dry and crumbly, add a little water; if it is too wet, add more masa harina. If you do not manage to flatten the ball of dough into a neat circle the first time, just re-roll it and try again.*
> • *An alternative to rolling out rounds of tortilla dough with a rolling pin is to use a tortilla press. Open the press and line both sides with sheets of clear film (plastic wrap). Shape the tortilla dough into balls, put one ball on the press and bring the top down firmly to flatten it into a neat round. Open the press, peel off the top layer of clear film and, using the bottom layer, lift the tortilla out of the press. Peel off this layer of clear film and repeat the process with the other dough balls.*

Flour Tortillas

Home-made tortillas taste so good filled with barbecued vegetables. You can make them in advance and then reheat them to serve.

Makes about 14
225g/8oz/2 cups plain (all-purpose) flour

From the storecupboard
5ml/1 tsp salt
15ml/1 tbsp lard or white cooking fat

1 Sift the flour and salt into a large mixing bowl. Gradually rub in the lard or white cooking fat, using your fingertips, until the mixture resembles coarse breadcrumbs.

2 Gradually add 120ml/4fl oz/½ cup water and mix to a soft dough. Knead lightly, form into a ball, cover with a cloth and leave to rest for 15 minutes. Prepare the barbecue.

3 Carefully divide the dough into about 14 portions and form these portions into small balls. One by one, roll out each ball of dough on a lightly floured wooden board to a round measuring about 15cm/6in. Trim the rounds if necessary.

4 Heat an ungreased flat griddle or frying pan over a medium heat. Cook the tortillas for about 1½–2 minutes on each side. Turn over with a palette knife or metal spatula when the bottom begins to brown. Wrap in a clean dish towel to keep warm until ready to serve.

> **Cook's Tips**
> • *Make flour tortillas whenever masa harina is difficult to find. To keep them soft and pliable, make sure they are kept warm until ready to serve, and eat as soon as possible.*
> • *These flour tortillas can also be cooked in the oven at 150°C/300°F/Gas 2.*
> • *For a quorn filling, simply fry some quorn mince in oil with ½ chopped onion, 1 small red chilli, finely chopped, 1 crushed garlic clove, ground black pepper and fresh thyme.*

Corn Tortillas: Energy 92kcal/385kJ; Protein 2.4g; Carbohydrate 18.3g, of which sugars 0g; Fat 0.8g, of which saturates 0g; Cholesterol 0mg; Calcium 1mg; Fibre 0.6g; Sodium 0mg.
Flour Tortillas: Energy 254kcal/1074kJ; Protein 5.9g; Carbohydrate 48.6g, of which sugars 0.9g; Fat 5.4g, of which saturates 2g; Cholesterol 4mg; Calcium 88mg; Fibre 1.9g; Sodium 2mg.

Corn Griddle Cakes

Known as arepas, these griddle cakes are a staple bread in several Latin American countries. They are delicious filled with soft white cheese, as in this recipe, or simply eaten plain as an accompaniment. With their crisp crust and chewy interior, arepas make an unusual and tasty snack or accompaniment to a barbecue meal.

Makes 15
200g/7oz/1¾ cups masarepa (or masa harina)
200g/7oz fresh white cheese, such as queso fresco or mozzarella, roughly chopped

From the storecupboard
15ml/1 tbsp oil
2.5ml/½ tsp salt

1 Combine the masarepa or masa harina and salt in a bowl. Gradually stir in the 300ml/½ pint/1¼ cups water to make a soft dough, then set aside for about 20 minutes.

2 Divide the dough into 15 equal-sized balls, then, using your fingers, flatten each ball into a circle, approximately 1cm/½in thick. Prepare the barbecue.

3 Heat a large, heavy frying pan or flat griddle over a medium heat and add 5ml/1 tsp oil. Using kitchen paper, gently wipe the surface of the frying pan, leaving it just lightly greased.

4 Place five of the arepas in the frying pan or on the griddle. Cook for approximately 4 minutes, then flip over and cook for a further 4 minutes. The arepas should be lightly blistered on both sides.

5 Open the arepas and fill each with a few small pieces of fresh white cheese. Return to the pan to cook until the cheese begins to melt. Remove from the heat and keep warm.

6 Cook the remaining ten arepas in the same way, oiling the pan and wiping with kitchen paper in between batches, to ensure it is always lightly greased. Serve the arepas while still warm so that the melted cheese is soft and runny.

Pitta Bread

Soft, slightly bubbly pitta bread is a pleasure to make. It can be eaten in a variety of ways, such as Mediterranean-style, filled with salad or little chunks of tofu cooked on the barbecue, or it can be torn into pieces and dunked in savoury dips such as hummus or tzatziki.

Makes 12
500g/1¼lb/5 cups strong white bread flour, or half white and half wholemeal (whole-wheat)
12.5ml/2½ tsp easy-blend (rapid-rise) dried yeast

From the storecupboard
15ml/1 tbsp olive oil
15ml/1 tbsp salt
30ml/2 tbsp vegetable oil

1 Combine the flour, yeast and salt. Combine the oil and 250ml/8fl oz/1 cup water, then add half of the flour mixture, stirring in the same direction, until the dough is stiff. Knead in the remaining flour. Place the dough in a clean bowl, cover with a clean dish towel and leave in a warm place for at least 30 minutes and up to 2 hours.

2 Knead the dough for 10 minutes, or until smooth. Lightly oil the bowl, place the dough in it, cover again and leave to rise in a warm place for about 1 hour, or until doubled in size.

3 Divide the dough into 12 equal pieces. With lightly floured hands, flatten each piece, then roll out into a round measuring about 20cm/8in and about 4mm–1cm/¼–½in thick. Keep the rolled breads covered while you make the remaining pittas.

4 Heat a heavy frying pan over a medium-high heat. When hot, lay one piece of flattened dough in the pan and cook for 15–20 seconds. Turn over and cook for about 1 minute.

5 When large bubbles start to form on the bread, turn it over again. It should puff up. Using a clean dish towel, gently press on the bread where the bubbles have formed. Cook for a total of 3 minutes, then remove the pitta from the pan. Repeat with the remaining dough. Wrap the pitta breads in a clean dish towel, stacking them as each one is cooked. Serve the pittas hot while they are soft and moist.

Corn Griddle Cakes: Energy 86kcal/363kJ; Protein 3.7g; Carbohydrate 10.4g, of which sugars 0.2g; Fat 3.6g, of which saturates 2g; Cholesterol 8mg; Calcium 67mg; Fibre 0.4g; Sodium 53mg.
Pitta Bread: Energy 150kcal/638kJ; Protein 3.9g; Carbohydrate 32.4g, of which sugars 0.6g; Fat 1.5g, of which saturates 0.2g; Cholesterol 0mg; Calcium 58mg; Fibre 1.3g; Sodium 493mg.

Sweet Cucumber Cooler

This sweet dipping sauce is good served with Thai bites.

Makes 120ml/4fl oz/½ cup
¼ small cucumber,
   thinly sliced
30ml/2 tbsp sugar

15ml/1 tbsp rice or white
   wine vinegar
2 shallots or 1 small red onion,
   thinly sliced

From the storecupboard
2.5ml/½ tsp salt

1 With a sharp knife, cut the cucumber slices into quarters.

2 Measure 75ml/5 tbsp water, the sugar, salt and vinegar into a stainless-steel or enamel pan, bring to the boil and simmer for less than 1 minute until the sugar has dissolved. Allow to cool. Add the cucumber and shallots. Serve at room temperature.

Sour Cucumber with Fresh Dill

This is half pickle, half salad, and totally delicious served with pumpernickel or other coarse, dark, full-flavoured bread. Choose smooth-skinned, smallish cucumbers as larger ones tend to be less tender, with tough skins and bitter seeds. If you can only buy a large cucumber, peel it before slicing.

Serves 4
2 small cucumbers, thinly sliced
3 onions, thinly sliced
75–90ml/5–6 tbsp cider vinegar
30–45ml/2–3 tbsp chopped
   fresh dill

From the storecupboard
salt and ground black pepper

1 Combine together the thinly sliced cucumbers and the thinly sliced onions. Season and toss together until thoroughly combined. Leave to stand in a cool place for 5–10 minutes.

2 Add the cider vinegar, 30–45ml/2–3 tbsp water and the chopped fresh dill to the cucumber and onion mixture. Toss all the ingredients together until well combined, then chill in the refrigerator for a few hours, or until ready to serve.

Jicama, Chilli and Lime Salad

A very tasty, crisp vegetable, the jicama is sometimes called the Mexican potato. Unlike potato, however, it can be eaten raw and here it is transformed into a zingy salad appetizer to serve with drinks.

Serves 4
1 jicama
2 fresh serrano chillies
2 limes

From the storecupboard
2.5ml/½ tsp salt

1 Peel the jicama with a potato peeler or knife, then cut it into 2cm/¾in cubes. Put the cubes in a large bowl, add the salt and toss well to coat.

2 Cut the serrano chillies in half, scrape out the seeds with a sharp knife, then cut the flesh into fine strips, taking care not to burn yourself with the chilli flesh. Grate the rind of one of the limes thinly, removing only the coloured part of the skin, then cut the lime in half and squeeze the juice.

3 Add the chillies, lime rind and juice to the jicama and mix thoroughly to ensure that all the jicama cubes are coated. Cut the other lime into wedges.

4 Cover the salad and chill for at least 1 hour before serving garnished with lime wedges. If the salad is to be served as an appetizer with drinks, transfer the jicama cubes to little bowls and offer them with cocktail sticks (toothpicks) for spearing.

Cook's Tips
• Look for jicama in Asian supermarkets, as it is widely used in Chinese cooking. It goes by several names and you may find it labelled as either yam bean or Chinese turnip.
• Take care when handling fresh chillies as the juice can burn sensitive skin. Wear rubber gloves to protect your hands or wash your hands very thoroughly after preparation. Be careful also not to touch your eyes when preparing chillies as the juices can cause unpleasant stinging.

Cucumber Cooler: Energy 147kcal/624kJ; Protein 1.4g; Carbohydrate 37.2g, of which sugars 35.8g; Fat 0.2g, of which saturates 0g; Cholesterol 0mg; Calcium 44mg; Fibre 1.3g; Sodium 6mg
Sour Cucumber and Dill: Energy 59kcal/243kJ; Protein 2.5g; Carbohydrate 11.7g, of which sugars 8.7g; Fat 0.5g, of which saturates 0g; Cholesterol 0mg; Calcium 72mg; Fibre 2.9g; Sodium 11mg.
Jicama, Chilli and Lime: Energy 73kcal/308kJ; Protein 2.1g; Carbohydrate 16.2g, of which sugars 1.4g; Fat 0.4g, of which saturates 0.1g; Cholesterol 0mg; Calcium 10mg; Fibre 1g; Sodium 12mg.

Beetroot with Fresh Mint

This simple and decorative beetroot salad can be served as part of a selection of salads, as an appetizer, or as an accompaniment to a main dish. Balsamic vinegar is a rich, dark vinegar with a mellow, deep flavour. It can be used to dress a variety of salad ingredients and is particularly good drizzled over a fresh tomato and basil salad.

Serves 4
4–6 cooked beetroot (beet)
15–30ml/1–2 tbsp balsamic
    vinegar
1 bunch fresh mint, leaves
    stripped and thinly shredded

From the storecupboard
30ml/2 tbsp olive oil
salt and ground black pepper

1 Slice the beetroot or cut into even dice with a sharp knife. Put the beetroot in a bowl. Add the balsamic vinegar, olive oil and a pinch of salt and pepper and toss together to combine.

2 Add half the thinly shredded fresh mint to the salad and toss lightly until thoroughly combined.

3 Place the salad in the refrigerator and chill for about 1 hour. Serve garnished with the remaining thinly shredded mint leaves.

> **Cook's Tip**
> Beetroot is well known for its medicinal qualities. It can be used to treat disorders of the blood, including anaemia. It is also an effective detoxifier and, because of its high fibre content, it also relieves constipation.

> **Variation**
> To make Tunisian beetroot, add a little harissa to taste and substitute chopped fresh coriander (cilantro) for the shredded mint.

Grated Beetroot and Yogurt Salad

With its beneficial nutritional properties, yogurt makes a tasty dip combined with mashed or grated ingredients, and mixed with a little vinegar or lemon juice it is good spooned as a sauce over grilled or fried vegetables. The most famous of the yogurt dips is the one with smoked aubergine, but there are a few other gems that get little mention, such as this one made with grated beetroot. Spiked with garlic and a pretty shade of pink, it is very moreish scooped on to flatbread or chunks of a warm, crusty loaf.

Serves 4
4 raw beetroot (beets), washed
    and trimmed
500g/1¼ lb/2¼ cups thick and
    creamy natural (plain) yogurt
2 garlic cloves, crushed
a few fresh mint leaves, shredded,
    to garnish

From the storecupboard
salt and ground black pepper

1 Boil the beetroot in plenty of water for 35–40 minutes until tender, but not mushy or soft. Drain and refresh under cold running water, then peel off the skins and grate the beetroot on to a plate. Squeeze it lightly with your fingers to drain off excess water.

2 In a bowl, beat the yogurt with the garlic and season with salt and pepper. Add the beetroot, reserving a little to garnish the top, and mix well. Garnish with mint leaves.

> **Variations**
> • In some households, the beetroot is diced and stir-fried with coriander seeds, sugar and a splash of apple vinegar. Then it is served warm with the cooling garlic-flavoured yogurt and garnished with dill.
> • Cut four carrots into chunks and steam for about 15 minutes, until they are tender but still with some bite, then grate and mix with the yogurt and garlic. Season with salt and pepper and garnish with mint or dill.

Beetroot with Fresh Mint: Energy 90kcal/378kJ; Protein 1.7g; Carbohydrate 8.9g, of which sugars 8.3g; Fat 5.6g, of which saturates 0.8g; Cholesterol 0mg; Calcium 21mg; Fibre 1.9g; Sodium 66mg.
Beetroot and Yogurt: Energy 95kcal/403kJ; Protein 7.8g; Carbohydrate 14.4g, of which sugars 13g; Fat 1.4g, of which saturates 0.6g; Cholesterol 2mg; Calcium 249mg; Fibre 1.3g; Sodium 137mg.

Globe Artichokes with Green Beans and Garlic Dressing

Piquant garlic dressing or creamy aioli go perfectly with these lightly cooked vegetables. Serve lemon wedges with the artichokes so that their juice may be squeezed over to taste. The vegetables can also be garnished with finely shredded lemon rind.

Serves 4–6
225g/8oz green beans
3 small globe artichokes
250ml/8fl oz/1 cup garlic
　dressing or aioli

From the storecupboard
15ml/1 tbsp lemon-flavoured
　olive oil
salt and ground black pepper

1 Cook the beans in boiling water for 1–2 minutes, until slightly softened. Drain well.

2 Trim the artichoke stalks close to the base. Cook them in a large pan of salted water for about 30 minutes, or until you can easily pull away a leaf from the base. Drain well.

3 Using a sharp knife, halve them lengthways and ease out their chokes using a teaspoon.

4 Arrange the artichokes and green beans on serving plates and drizzle with the oil. Season with coarse salt and a little pepper. Spoon the garlic dressing or aioli into the hearts and serve warm.

5 To eat the artichokes, pull the leaves from the base one at a time and use to scoop a little of the dressing. It is only the fleshy end of each leaf that is eaten as well as the base, bottom or 'fond'.

Cook's Tip
Artichokes should feel heavy for their size. When selecting, make sure that the inner leaves are wrapped tightly round the choke and the heart inside.

Halloumi and Grape Salad

Firm and salty halloumi cheese is a great standby ingredient for turning a simple salad into a special dish. In this recipe it is tossed with sweet, juicy grapes, which complement its flavour and texture. Fresh young thyme leaves and dill taste especially good mixed with the salad. Serve with a crusty walnut or sun-dried tomato bread for a light lunch.

Serves 4
150g/5oz mixed salad leaves and
　tender fresh herb sprigs
175g/6oz mixed seedless green
　and black grapes
250g/9oz halloumi cheese
75ml/5 tbsp oil and lemon
　juice or vinegar dressing

1 Toss together the salad leaves and fresh herb sprigs and the green and black grapes, then transfer to a large serving plate.

2 Thinly slice the halloumi cheese. Heat a large non-stick frying pan. Add the sliced halloumi cheese and cook briefly until it just starts to turn golden brown on the underside.

3 Turn the cheese with a fish slice or metal spatula and cook the other side until it is golden brown.

4 Arrange the fried cheese over the salad on the serving plate. Pour over the oil and lemon juice, or vinegar, dressing and serve immediately while the cheese is still hot with some warm crusty bread.

Variation
Make this halloumi and grape salad really special with a fresh and tangy orange and tarragon dressing. In a small bowl, whisk together the rind and juice of 1 large orange with 45ml/3 tbsp olive oil and 15ml/1 tbsp chopped fresh tarragon. Season with salt and plenty of ground black pepper to taste.

Globe Artichokes: Energy 299kcal/1232kJ; Protein 1.1g; Carbohydrate 1.7g, of which sugars 1.4g; Fat 22.7g, of which saturates 4.5g; Cholesterol 0mg; Calcium 39mg; Fibre 1.4g; Sodium 418mg.
Halloumi and Grape: Energy 235kcal/974kJ; Protein 8g; Carbohydrate 2.8g, of which sugars 2.8g; Fat 21.4g, of which saturates 7.6g; Cholesterol 24mg; Calcium 160mg; Fibre 0.3g; Sodium 166mg.

Orange and Chicory Salad with Walnuts

Chicory and oranges are both winter ingredients, so this salad is perfect as a light accompaniment to hearty winter dishes.

Serves 6
2 chicory (Belgian endive) heads
2 oranges
25g/1oz/2 tbsp walnut halves, roughly chopped

From the storecupboard
30ml/2 tbsp extra-virgin olive oil
salt and ground black pepper

1 Trim off the bottom of each chicory head and separate the leaves. Arrange on a serving platter.

2 Place one of the oranges on a chopping board and slice off the top and bottom to expose the flesh. Place the orange upright and, using a small sharp knife, slice down between the skin and the flesh. Do this all the way around to remove all peel and pith. Repeat with the remaining orange, reserving any juice.

3 Holding one orange over a bowl to catch the juices, cut between the membrane to release the segments. Repeat with the second orange. Arrange the orange segments on the platter with the chicory.

4 Whisk the oil with any juice from the oranges, and season with salt and pepper to taste. Sprinkle the walnuts over the salad, drizzle over the dressing and serve immediately.

Cook's Tip
Blood oranges look especially attractive served in this dish.

Variation
Use young spinach leaves or rocket (arugula) instead of chicory.

Watercress Salad with Pear and Blue Cheese Dressing

A refreshing light salad, this dish combines lovely peppery watercress, soft juicy pears and a tart dressing. Dunsyre Blue cheese from Lanarkshire, Scotland, has a wonderfully sharp flavour with a crumbly texture, but other blue cheeses can be substituted.

Serves 4
25g/1oz Dunsyre Blue cheese
15ml/1 tbsp lemon juice
2 bunches watercress, thoroughly washed and trimmed
2 ripe pears

From the storecupboard
30ml/2 tbsp walnut oil
salt and ground black pepper

1 Crumble the Dunsyre Blue into a bowl, then mash into the walnut oil, using a fork.

2 Whisk in the lemon juice to create a thickish mixture. If you need to thicken it further, add a little more cheese. Season to taste with salt and ground black pepper.

3 Arrange a pile of watercress on the sides of four plates.

4 Peel and slice the two pears, then place the pear slices to the side of the watercress, allowing half a pear per person. Drizzle the dressing over the salad. The salad is best served immediately at room temperature.

Cook's Tips
• *Choose ripe Comice or similar pears that are soft and juicy.*
• *If you want to get things ready in advance, peel and slice the pears, then rub with some lemon juice; this will stop them discolouring so quickly.*

Variation
For a milder, tangy dressing use Dolcelatte cheese instead.

Watercress and Blue Cheese: Energy 106kcal/442kJ; Protein 2.3g; Carbohydrate 7.6g, of which sugars 7.6g; Fat 7.6g, of which saturates 1.8g; Cholesterol 5mg; Calcium 81mg; Fibre 2g; Sodium 91mg.
Orange and Chicory: Energy 81kcal/335kJ; Protein 1.2g; Carbohydrate 4.6g, of which sugars 3.9g; Fat 6.8g, of which saturates 0.8g; Cholesterol 0mg; Calcium 31mg; Fibre 1.2g; Sodium 3mg.

Watermelon and Feta Salad

The combination of sweet watermelon with salty feta cheese is inspired by Turkish tradition. The salad may be served plain and light, on a leafy base, or with a herbed vinaigrette dressing drizzled over. It is perfect served as an appetizer. Feta cheese is salty because it is preserved in brine – but the salt is not supposed to overpower the taste of the cheese.

Serves 4
4 slices watermelon, chilled
130g/4½ oz feta cheese,
preferably sheep's milk feta, cut
into bitesize pieces
handful of mixed seeds, such as
lightly toasted pumpkin seeds
and sunflower seeds
10–15 black olives

1 Cut the rind off the watermelon and remove as many seeds as possible. Cut the flesh into triangular-shaped chunks.

2 Mix the watermelon, feta cheese, mixed seeds and black olives. Cover and chill the salad for 30 minutes before serving.

Cook's Tips
• *The best choice of olives for this recipe are plump black Mediterranean ones, such as kalamata. Alternatively, use any other shiny, brined varieties or dry-cured black olives.*
• *The nutty flavour and crunchy texture of toasted seeds gives an instant healthy boost to this dish. Sunflower seeds are rich in Vitamin E and pumpkin seeds are high in iron and zinc.*

Variations
• *Exchange watermelon for juicy ripe figs in this recipe.*
• *An alternative equally refreshing way with the appetizing feta cheese is in a classic Greek salad. This distinctive salad is served with juicy ripe tomatoes, crunchy cucumber, onion and plump olives.*

Tomato, Bean and Fried Basil Salad

Infusing basil in hot oil brings out its wonderful, aromatic flavour, which works so well in almost any tomato dish. Various canned beans or chickpeas can be used instead of mixed beans in this simple dish, as they all taste good and make a wholesome salad to serve as an accompaniment or a satisfying snack with some warm, grainy bread.

Serves 4
15g/½ oz/½ cup fresh basil leaves
300g/11oz cherry
tomatoes, halved
400g/14oz can mixed beans,
drained and rinsed

From the storecupboard
75ml/5 tbsp extra virgin olive oil
salt and ground black pepper

1 Reserve one-third of the basil leaves for garnish, then tear the remainder into pieces. Pour the olive oil into a small pan. Add the torn basil and heat gently for 1 minute, until the basil sizzles and begins to colour.

2 Place the halved cherry tomatoes and beans in a bowl. Pour in the basil oil and add a little salt and plenty of ground black pepper. Toss the ingredients together gently, cover and leave to marinate at room temperature for at least 30 minutes. Serve the salad sprinkled with the remaining basil leaves.

Pink Grapefruit and Avocado Salad

Smooth, creamy avocado and zesty citrus fruit are perfect partners in an attractive, refreshing salad. Pink grapefruit are tangy but not too sharp, or use large oranges for a sweeter flavour. Avocados turn brown quickly when exposed to the air: the acidic grapefruit juice will prevent this, so combine the ingredients as soon as the avocados have been sliced.

Serves 4
2 pink grapefruit
2 ripe avocados
90g/3½ oz rocket (arugula)

From the storecupboard
30ml/2 tbsp chilli oil
salt and ground black pepper

1 Slice the top and bottom off a grapefruit, then cut off all the peel and pith from around the side. Working over a small bowl to catch the juices, cut out the segments from between the membranes and place them in a separate bowl. Squeeze any juices remaining in the membranes into the bowl, then discard them. Repeat with the remaining grapefruit.

2 Halve, stone (pit) and peel the avocados. Slice the flesh and add it to the grapefruit segments. Whisk a little salt and then the chilli oil into the grapefruit juice.

3 Pile the rocket leaves on to four serving plates and top with the grapefruit segments and avocado. Pour over the dressing and serve.

Watermelon and Feta: Energy 256kcal/1066kJ; Protein 7.7g; Carbohydrate 12.9g, of which sugars 11.6g; Fat 19.7g, of which saturates 6.2g; Cholesterol 23mg; Calcium 165mg; Fibre 1.4g; Sodium 616mg.
Tomato and Basil: Energy 404kcal/1701kJ; Protein 22.8g; Carbohydrate 46.5g, of which sugars 4.9g; Fat 15.4g, of which saturates 2.3g; Cholesterol 0mg; Calcium 113mg; Fibre 16.7g; Sodium 26mg.
Pink Grapefruit and Avocado: Energy 151kcal/625kJ; Protein 1.1g; Carbohydrate 5.6g, of which sugars 5.2g; Fat 13.9g, of which saturates 2.4g; Cholesterol 0mg; Calcium 24mg; Fibre 1.9g; Sodium 13mg.

Moroccan Carrot Salad

In this intriguing salad from North Africa, the carrots are lightly cooked before being tossed in a cumin and coriander vinaigrette. Cumin is widely used in Indian and Mexican cooking, as well as North African cuisines. It has a strong and spicy aroma and a warm pungent flavour that goes particularly well with root vegetables. This salad is a perfect accompaniment for both everyday or special meals.

Serves 4–6
3–4 carrots, thinly sliced
1.5ml/¼ tsp ground cumin, or to taste
60ml/4 tbsp garlic-flavoured oil and vinegar dressing
30ml/2 tbsp chopped fresh coriander (cilantro) leaves or a mixture of coriander and parsley

From the storecupboard
salt and ground black pepper

1 Cook the thinly sliced carrots by either steaming or boiling in lightly salted water until they are just tender but not soft. Drain the carrots, leave for a few minutes to dry and cool, then put into a mixing bowl.

2 Add the cumin, garlic dressing and herbs. Season to taste and chill well before serving. Check the seasoning just before serving and add more ground cumin, salt or black pepper, if required.

> **Variation**
> *Raw young tender turnips have a tangy, slightly peppery flavour and make another excellent side salad. Serve as an accompaniment for grilled poultry or meat. It is also delicious as a light appetizer, garnished with parsley and paprika, and served with warmed flatbreads such as pitta or naan. To make, thinly slice or coarsely grate 2–4 young turnips. Alternatively, thinly slice half the turnips and grate the remaining half. Put in a bowl. Add ¼–½ a finely chopped onion and 2–3 drops white wine vinegar and season to taste. Toss together, then stir in 60–90ml/4–6 tbsp sour cream. Chill well before serving.*

Date, Orange and Carrot Salad

Take exotic fresh dates and marry them with everyday ingredients, such as carrots and oranges, to make this deliciously different salad. The salad looks really pretty arranged on a base of sweet Little Gem lettuce leaves.

Serves 4
3 carrots
3 oranges
115g/4oz/scant ¾ cup fresh dates, stoned (pitted) and cut lengthways into eighths
25g/1oz/¼ cup toasted whole almonds, chopped

From the storecupboard
salt and ground black pepper

1 Grate the carrots and place in a mound in a serving dish, or on four individual plates.

2 Peel and segment two of the oranges and arrange the orange segments around the carrot. Season with salt and ground black pepper. Pile the dates on top, then sprinkle with the chopped, toasted almonds.

3 Squeeze the juice from the remaining orange and sprinkle it over the salad. Chill in the refrigerator for an hour before serving.

> **Cook's Tips**
> • *Dates should be plump and glossy. Medjool dates have a wrinkly skin, but most other varieties are smooth. They can be stored in the refrigerator for up to a week.*
> • *There are two types of almond: sweet and bitter. The best sweet varieties come from Spain – they are the flat and slender Jodan almonds and the heart-shaped Valencia almonds, which are also grown in Portugal – and the flatter Californian almonds. For the best flavour, buy the almonds shelled, but still in their skins. Then blanch them yourself by covering with boiling water, leaving for a few minutes, then draining and slipping off the skins.*

Date, Orange and Carrot: Energy 138kcal/582kJ; Protein 3.6g; Carbohydrate 21.8g, of which sugars 21.4g; Fat 4.7g, of which saturates 0.4g; Cholesterol 0mg; Calcium 90mg; Fibre 3.9g; Sodium 18mg.
Moroccan Carrot: Energy 53kcal/220kJ; Protein 0.6g; Carbohydrate 4.2g, of which sugars 3.9g; Fat 3.9g, of which saturates 0.6g; Cholesterol 0mg; Calcium 29mg; Fibre 1.6g; Sodium 15mg.

Grilled Baby Artichokes

This is an enjoyable way to eat artichokes. Just hold the skewer with the artichoke in one hand, tear off a leaf with the other and dip that into the hot melted butter.

Serves 6
12 baby artichokes with stalks, about 1.3kg/3lb total weight

1 lemon, halved
2 garlic cloves, crushed with a pinch of salt
15ml/1 tbsp chopped fresh flat leaf parsley

From the storecupboard
200g/7oz/scant 1 cup butter
salt and ground black pepper

1 Soak 12 wooden skewers in cold water for 30 minutes. Drain, then skewer a baby artichoke on to each one. Bring a large pan of salted water to the boil. Squeeze the juice of one lemon half, and add it, with the lemon shell, to the pan.

2 Place the artichokes head first into the pan and boil for 5–8 minutes, or until just tender. Drain well. Set aside for up to 1 hour or use immediately.

3 Prepare the barbecue. Put the butter, garlic and parsley into a small pan and squeeze in the juice of the remaining half-lemon.

4 Position a lightly oiled grill rack over the coals to heat over medium heat. If the artichokes have been allowed to cool, wrap the heads in foil and place them on the grill for 3 minutes, then unwrap and return to the heat for 1 minute, turning frequently. If they are still hot, grill without the foil for 4 minutes, turning often.

5 When the artichokes are almost ready, melt the butter sauce in the pan on the barbecue. Either transfer the sauce to six small serving bowls or pour a little on to each plate. Serve it with the artichokes on their skewers.

> **Cook's Tip**
> Have plenty of napkins on hand to catch any stray drops of butter sauce.

Roasted Red Peppers with Feta, Capers and Preserved Lemons

Red peppers, particularly the long, slim, horn-shaped variety, feature widely in the cooking of North Africa and the Middle East. Roasting them really brings out their smoky flavour and they taste wonderful with crumbled white cheese. Feta is suggested here, but you can use any salty crumbly cheese. This dish makes a great mezze.

Serves 4
4 fleshy red (bell) peppers
200g/7oz feta cheese, crumbled
30ml/2 tbsp capers, drained
peel of 1 preserved lemon, cut into small pieces

From the storecupboard
30–45ml/2–3 tbsp olive oil or argan oil
salt

1 Preheat the grill (broiler) on the hottest setting. Roast the red peppers under the grill, turning frequently, until they soften and their skins begin to blacken. (Alternatively, spear the peppers, one at a time, on long metal skewers and turn them over a gas flame, or roast them in a very hot oven.)

2 Place the peppers in a plastic bag, seal and leave them to stand for 15 minutes. Peel the peppers, remove and discard the stalks and seeds and then slice the flesh and arrange on a plate.

3 Add the crumbled feta and pour over the olive or argan oil. Scatter the capers and preserved lemon over the top and sprinkle with a little salt, if required (this depends on whether the feta is salty or not). Serve with chunks of bread to mop up the delicious, oil-rich juices.

> **Cook's Tip**
> Argan oil originates in Morocco and is made from the fruit of the argan tree. It has a distinctive nutty flavour, so if you can't find it, use another nutty oil.

Grilled Baby Artichokes 263kcal/1084kJ; Protein 1.4g; Carbohydrate 2.5g, of which sugars 1.2g; Fat 27.7g, of which saturates 17.4g; Cholesterol 71mg; Calcium 49mg; Fibre 1.4g; Sodium 262mg.
Peppers with Feta: Energy 255kcal/1058kJ; Protein 9.6g; Carbohydrate 12g, of which sugars 11.4g; Fat 19.1g, of which saturates 8.2g; Cholesterol 35mg; Calcium 194mg; Fibre 2.8g; Sodium 727mg.

Warm Halloumi and Fennel Salad

The firm rubbery texture of halloumi cheese makes it perfect for the barbecue, as it keeps its shape very well. It is widely available in most large supermarkets and Greek delicatessens.

Serves 4

200g/7oz halloumi cheese, thickly sliced

2 fennel bulbs, trimmed and thinly sliced

30ml/2 tbsp roughly chopped fresh oregano

From the storecupboard

45ml/3 tbsp lemon-infused olive oil

salt and ground black pepper

1 Put the halloumi, fennel and oregano in a bowl and drizzle over the lemon-infused oil. Season with salt and black pepper to taste. (Halloumi is a fairly salty cheese, so be very careful when adding extra salt.)

2 Cover the bowl with clear film (plastic wrap) and chill for about 2 hours to allow the flavours to develop.

3 Place the halloumi and fennel on a griddle pan or over the barbecue, reserving the marinade, and cook for about 3 minutes on each side, until charred.

4 Divide the halloumi and fennel among four serving plates and drizzle over the reserved marinade. Serve immediately.

Cook's Tips
• To make your own lemon-flavoured oil, finely pare the rind from 1 lemon, place on kitchen paper, and leave to dry for 1 day. Add the dried rind to a bottle of olive oil and leave to infuse (steep) for up to 3 days. Strain into a clean bottle and discard the rind.
• Other flavoured oils would work well in this dish, such as herb oils, but take care with chilli or garlic which can be overpowering.

Pear and Blue Cheese Salad

A juicy variety of pear, such as a Williams, is just perfect in this dish. You can use any other blue cheese, such as Stilton or Gorgonzola, in place of the Roquefort, if you prefer.

Serves 4

4 ripe pears

115g/4oz Roquefort cheese

15ml/1 tbsp balsamic vinegar

From the storecupboard

30ml/2 tbsp olive oil

salt and ground black pepper

1 Cut the pears into quarters and remove the cores. Thinly slice each pear quarter and arrange on a serving platter.

2 Slice the Roquefort as thinly as possible and place over the pears. Mix the oil and vinegar together and drizzle over the pears. Season with salt and pepper and serve.

Cook's Tip
Rich, dark balsamic vinegar has an intense yet mellow flavour. It is produced in Modena in the north of Italy and is widely available in most supermarkets. Sherry vinegar could be used as a substitute, it is mellow but slightly less intense.

Variations
• Try substituting soft ripe juicy figs for the pears in this salad dish and use walnut oil to replace the olive oil. The combination of exotic flavoured figs and tangy blue cheese with a hint of nuttiness is exquisite.
• Add 115g/4oz/1 cup shelled walnut halves to the recipe to give a great crunch. Make it into a more complete meal with a bed of soft mixed salad leaves.
• Alternatively, boil some dried pasta shapes, such as penne, according to the packet instructions, drain well and cool. Place some salad leaves in a bowl, pile the pasta on top of the salad, sprinkle over crumbled Roquefort, pour over a dressing and add some walnut halves. Toss and serve.

Halloumi and Fennel: Energy 215kcal/889kJ; Protein 10.2g; Carbohydrate 1.8g, of which sugars 1.7g; Fat 18.6g, of which saturates 8.1g; Cholesterol 29mg; Calcium 205mg; Fibre 2.4g; Sodium 209mg.
Pear and Blue Cheese: Energy 208kcal/865kJ; Protein 6.4g; Carbohydrate 15g, of which sugars 15g; Fat 14g, of which saturates 6.3g; Cholesterol 22mg; Calcium 157mg; Fibre 3.3g; Sodium 355mg.

Grilled Strawberries and Marshmallows

It is always a treat to have permission to eat marshmallows. After cooking, dredge these little kebabs with loads of icing sugar, some of which will melt into the strawberry juice. The grill has to be very hot to sear the marshmallows quickly before they melt.

Serves 4

16 mixed pink and white vegetarian marshmallows, chilled
16 strawberries
icing (confectioners') sugar for dusting
8 short lengths of cherry wood or metal skewers

1 Prepare the barbecue. If you are using cherry wood skewers, soak them in water for 30 minutes. Position a lightly oiled grill rack just above the hot coals to heat.

2 Spike two marshmallows and two strawberries on each drained cherry wood or metal skewer and grill over the hot coals for 20 seconds on each side. If nice grill marks don't appear easily, don't persist for too long or the marshmallows may burn – cook until they are warm to the touch and only just beginning to melt.

3 Transfer the skewered strawberries and marshmallows to individual dessert plates or a large platter, dust generously with icing sugar and serve.

Cook's Tip
By chilling the marshmallows for at least half an hour, they will be firmer and easier to thread on to the skewers.

Variation
For pure indulgence, serve these skewers with a chocolate fondue. Combine plain (semisweet) chocolate, cream and alcohol (optional) in a fondue pan and heat until melted.

Honey-seared Melon

This fabulously simple dessert can be made with melon that is slightly underripe, because the honeycomb will sweeten it up beautifully.

Serves 6

1.3kg/3lb melon, preferably Charentais
200g/7oz honeycomb
a bunch of lavender, plus extra flowers for decoration
300g/11oz/2 cups raspberries

1 Prepare the barbecue. Cut the melon in half, scoop out the seeds, then cut each half into three slices. Put a third of the honeycomb in a bowl and dilute by stirring in 5ml/1 tsp water. Make a brush with the lavender and dip it into the honey.

2 Heat a griddle on the grill rack over hot coals. Lightly brush the melon with the honey mixture. Grill for 30 seconds on each side. Serve hot, sprinkled with the raspberries and remaining lavender flowers, and topped with the remaining honeycomb.

Melon with Grilled Strawberries

Sprinkling the strawberries with a little sugar, then grilling them, helps bring out their flavour. Serve with ice cream or lemon sorbet.

Serves 4

115g/4oz/1 cup strawberries
15ml/1 tbsp icing (confectioners') sugar, plus extra for dusting
½ cantaloupe melon

1 Soak four wooden skewers in water. Meanwhile, scoop out the seeds from the half melon. Using a sharp knife, remove the skin, then cut the flesh into wedges and arrange on a plate.

2 Preheat the grill (broiler). Hull the strawberries and cut in half, arrange cut side up on a baking sheet and dust with icing sugar.

3 Thread the strawberry halves on to skewers, place on a grill rack and grill (broil) on high for 3–4 minutes or until the sugar starts to bubble and turn golden. Remove from the skewers and sprinkle over the melon slices, dusting with the remaining icing sugar.

Strawberries and Marshmallows: Energy 110kcal/466kJ; Protein 1.4g; Carbohydrate 27.6g, of which sugars 22.9g; Fat 0.1g, of which saturates 0g; Cholesterol 0mg; Calcium 11mg; Fibre 0.5g; Sodium 10mg.
Honey-seared Melon: Energy 113kcal/480kJ; Protein 1.9g; Carbohydrate 27.2g, of which sugars 27.2g; Fat 0.4g, of which saturates 0.1g; Cholesterol 0mg; Calcium 42mg; Fibre 2.1g; Sodium 71mg.
Melon with Strawberries: Energy 46kcal/197kJ; Protein 1g; Carbohydrate 10.9g, of which sugars 10.9g; Fat 0.2g, of which saturates 0g; Cholesterol 0mg; Calcium 32mg; Fibre 1.6g; Sodium 12mg.

Calvados-flamed Bananas

Soft and creamy baked bananas, flamed with calvados, are delicious served with a rich butterscotch sauce. The sauce can be made in advance and the bananas are quickly cooked. Have a sensible person ignite the calvados, which makes a spectacular end to a meal.

Serves 6
115g/4oz/generous ½ cup sugar
150ml/¼ pint/⅔ cup double
 (heavy) cream
6 large slightly underripe bananas
90ml/6 tbsp calvados

From the storecupboard
25g/1oz/2 tbsp butter

1 Place the sugar and 150ml/¼ pint/⅔ cup water in a large pan and heat gently until the sugar has dissolved. Increase the heat and boil until the mixture turns a rich golden caramel colour.

2 Remove from the heat and carefully add the butter and cream; the mixture will foam up in the pan. Replace it over a gentle heat and stir to a smooth sauce, then pour into a bowl and leave to cool. Cover and chill until needed.

3 Prepare the barbecue. Wrap the bananas individually in foil. Position a grill rack over the hot coals. Grill the wrapped bananas over high heat for 10 minutes.

4 Transfer the bananas to a tray, open up the parcels and slit the upper side of each banana skin.

5 Meanwhile, gently warm the calvados in a small pan, then pour some into each banana. Put them back on the barbecue and wait for a few seconds before carefully igniting the calvados with a long match. Serve with the sauce as soon as the flames die down.

> **Cook's Tip**
> *These bananas can be cooked indoors using a grill (broiler) or by baking them in a hot oven.*

Baked Bananas with Ice Cream and Toffee Sauce

Bananas make one of the easiest of all desserts, just as welcome as a comforting winter treat as they are to follow a barbecue. For an extra sweet finishing touch, grate some plain chocolate on the bananas, over the sauce, just before serving. If baking on a barbecue, turn the bananas occasionally to ensure even cooking.

Serves 4
4 large bananas
75g/3oz/scant ½ cup light
 muscovado (brown) sugar
75ml/5 tbsp double
 (heavy) cream
4 scoops good-quality vanilla
 ice cream

1 Preheat the oven to 180°C/350°F/Gas 4. Put the unpeeled bananas in an ovenproof dish and bake for 15–20 minutes, until the skins are very dark and the flesh feels soft when squeezed.

2 Meanwhile, heat the light muscovado sugar in a small, heavy pan with 75ml/5 tbsp water until dissolved. Bring to the boil and add the double cream. Cook for 5 minutes, until the sauce has thickened and is toffee coloured. Remove from the heat.

3 Transfer the baked bananas in their skins to serving plates and split them lengthways to reveal the flesh. Pour some of the sauce over the bananas and top with scoops of vanilla ice cream. Serve any remaining sauce separately.

> **Variation**
> *A spicy vanilla butter adds a luxurious finish to this dessert. To make, split 6 green cardamom pods and remove seeds, crush lightly. Split a vanilla pod lengthways and scrape out the tiny seeds. Mix with cardamom seeds, finely grated rind and juice of small orange and 45ml/3 tbsp butter into a thick paste. Place a spoonful inside each baked banana.*

Calvados Bananas: Energy 359kcal/1501kJ; Protein 1.7g; Carbohydrate 43.7g, of which sugars 41.4g; Fat 17.2g, of which saturates 10.6g; Cholesterol 43mg; Calcium 29mg; Fibre 1.1g; Sodium 33mg.
Bananas/Ice Cream: Energy 455kcal/1910kJ; Protein 6.9g; Carbohydrate 63.2g, of which sugars 56.6g; Fat 21.1g, of which saturates 12.6g; Cholesterol 53mg; Calcium 215mg; Fibre 0.6g; Sodium 178mg.

Baked Apples with Marsala

The Marsala cooks down with the juice from the apples and the butter to make a rich, sticky sauce. Serve these delicious apples with a spoonful of extra-thick cream.

Serves 6
4 medium cooking apples
50g/2oz/⅓ cup ready-to-eat dried figs
150ml/¼ pint/⅔ cup Marsala

From the storecupboard
50g/2oz/¼ cup butter, softened

1 Preheat the oven to 180°C/350°F/Gas 4. Using an apple corer, remove the cores from the apples and discard.

2 Place the apples in a small, shallow baking pan and stuff the figs into the holes in the centre of each apple.

3 Top each apple with a quarter of the butter and pour over the Marsala. Cover the pan tightly with foil and bake for about 30 minutes.

4 Remove the foil from the apples and bake for a further 10 minutes, or until the apples are tender and the juices have reduced slightly. Serve immediately with any remaining pan juices drizzled over the top.

Cook's Tip
Marsala is an Italian fortified wine used to flavour desserts, including the infamous tiramisu. If you are unable to find Marsala, you could use a sweet sherry, such as Manzanilla, or Madeira wine. You could even use port, which would give an attractive pink colour to the dish.

Variation
Instead of dried figs, use raisins, sultanas (golden raisins), dried ready-to-eat apricots or cherries. For a crunchy version, add chopped hazelnuts or almonds.

Passion Fruit Soufflés

These simplified soufflés are so easy and work beautifully. The passion fruit adds a tropical note to a favourite classic. The soufflés look very pretty sprinkled with icing sugar.

Serves 4
200ml/7fl oz/scant 1 cup ready-made fresh custard
3 passion fruits, halved
2 egg whites

From the storecupboard
knob (pat) of softened butter, for greasing

1 Preheat the oven to 200°C/400°F/Gas 6. Grease four 200ml/7fl oz/scant 1 cup ramekin dishes with the butter.

2 Pour the custard into a large mixing bowl. Scrape out the seeds and juice from the halved passion fruit and stir into the custard until well combined.

3 Whisk the egg whites until stiff, and fold a quarter of them into the custard. Carefully fold in the remaining egg whites, then spoon the mixture into the ramekin dishes.

4 Place the dishes on a baking sheet and bake in the oven for 8–10 minutes, or until the soufflés are well risen. Serve immediately.

Cook's Tip
Despite their reputation, soufflés are not difficult to cook. Proper preparation of the cooking dishes is key to the success. If the dish is well greased, the soufflé will rise up the sides better.

Variation
Add a crunchy contrast to the soufflé by adding a layer of coarsely crushed biscuits (cookies) in the middle of the mixture before cooking. Italian amaretti would add a hint of almond, whereas crushed ginger biscuits would give a touch of spice.

Baked Apples/Marsala: Energy 134kcal/560kJ; Protein 0.5g; Carbohydrate 11.1g, of which sugars 11.1g; Fat 7g, of which saturates 4.3g; Cholesterol 18mg; Calcium 24mg; Fibre 1.3g; Sodium 57mg.
Passion Fruit Soufflés: Energy 59kcal/249kJ; Protein 3.1g; Carbohydrate 8.8g, of which sugars 7.1g; Fat 1g, of which saturates 0g; Cholesterol 1mg; Calcium 48mg; Fibre 0.4g; Sodium 53mg.

Grilled Peaches with Meringues

Ripe peaches take on a fabulous scented fruitiness when grilled with brown sugar, and mini meringues are the perfect accompaniment. Serve with crème fraîche flavoured with a little grated orange rind. When buying peaches or nectarines, choose fruit with an attractive rosy bloom, avoiding any that have a green-tinged skin or feel hard. Nectarines have a smoother skin than the furry peaches.

Serves 6
2 egg whites
115g/4oz/½ cup soft light brown sugar, reserving 5ml/1 tsp for the peaches
pinch of ground cinnamon
6 ripe peaches, or nectarines

1 Preheat the oven to 140°C/275°F/Gas 1. Line two large baking sheets with baking parchment.

2 Whisk the egg whites until they form stiff peaks. Gradually whisk in the sugar and ground cinnamon until the mixture is stiff and glossy. Pipe 18 very small meringues on to the trays and bake for 40 minutes. Leave in the oven to cool.

3 Meanwhile, halve and stone (pit) the peaches or nectarines, sprinkling each half with a little sugar as it is cut. Grill (broil) for 4–5 minutes, until just beginning to caramelize.

4 Arrange the grilled peaches on serving plates with the meringues and serve immediately.

Cook's Tip
Use leftover egg whites to make these little cinnamon-flavoured meringues. The meringues can be stored in an airtight container for about 2 weeks. Serve them after dinner with coffee or with desserts in place of biscuits (cookies).

Roast Peaches with Amaretto

This is an excellent dessert to serve in summer, when peaches are at their juiciest and most fragrant. The apricot and almond flavour of the amaretto liqueur subtly enhances the sweetness of the ripe peaches. Serve with a spoonful of crème fraîche or whipped cream.

Serves 4
4 ripe peaches
45ml/3 tbsp Amaretto di Sarone liqueur
45ml/3 tbsp clear honey

1 Preheat the oven 190°C/375°F/Gas 5. Cut the peaches in half and prise out the stones (pits) with the point of the knife.

2 Place the peaches cut side up in a roasting pan. In a small bowl, mix the amaretto liqueur with the honey, and drizzle over the halved peaches, covering them evenly.

3 Bake the peaches for 20–25 minutes, or until tender. Place two peach halves on each serving plate and drizzle with the pan juices. Serve immediately.

Cook's Tip
You can cook these peaches over a barbecue. Place them on sheets of foil, drizzle over liqueur, then scrunch the foil around them to seal. Cook for 15–20 minutes.

Variations
• Nectarines can be used in place of peaches for this recipe.
• Replace the Amaretto and honey with ground almonds and muscovado (brown) sugar, which will caramelize when roasted.
• Put a small cube of marzipan in the centre where the stone (pit) was and sprinkle with muscovado sugar.
• Serve with ice cream or Greek (US strained plain) yogurt.

Peaches with Meringues: Energy 107kcal/457kJ; Protein 1.9g; Carbohydrate 26.4g, of which sugars 26.4g; Fat 0.1g, of which saturates 0g; Cholesterol 0mg; Calcium 17mg; Fibre 1.3g; Sodium 22mg.
Peaches with Amaretto: Energy 91kcal/387kJ; Protein 1.1g; Carbohydrate 16.4g, of which sugars 16.4g; Fat 0.1g, of which saturates 0g; Cholesterol 0mg; Calcium 8mg; Fibre 1.5g; Sodium 2mg.

Summer Berries in Sabayon Glaze

This luxurious combination of summer berries under a light and fluffy liqueur sauce is lightly grilled to form a crisp, caramelized topping. Fresh or frozen berries can be used in this dessert. If you use frozen berries, defrost them in a sieve over a bowl to allow the juices to drip. Pour a little juice over the fruit before dividing among the dishes.

Serves 4

450g/1lb/4 cups mixed summer berries, or soft fruit

4 egg yolks

50g/2oz/¼ cup vanilla sugar or caster (superfine) sugar

120ml/4fl oz/½ cup liqueur, such as Cointreau or Kirsch, or a white dessert wine

1 Arrange the mixed summer berries or soft fruit in four individual flameproof dishes. Preheat the grill (broiler).

2 Whisk the yolks in a large bowl with the sugar and liqueur or wine. Place over a pan of hot water and whisk constantly until the mixture is thick, fluffy and pale. You should be able to form peaks in the sauce that hold their shape.

3 Pour equal quantities of the yolk mixture into each dish. Place under the grill for 1–2 minutes, until just turning brown. Add an extra splash of liqueur, if you like, and serve immediately.

Cook's Tip
To separate eggs, gently prise the two halves apart with your thumbs. Keep the yolk in one half and allow the white to drop into a bowl below. Slip the yolk from one to the other.

Variation
If you prefer, you can make a non-alcoholic version of this dish using cranberry juice or pomegranate, or any other full-flavoured fruit juice.

Baked Ricotta Cakes with Red Sauce

These honey-flavoured desserts take only minutes to make from a few ingredients. The fragrant fruity sauce provides a contrast of both colour and flavour. The red berry sauce can be made a day in advance and chilled until ready to use. Frozen fruit doesn't need extra water, as it usually yields its juice easily on thawing.

Serves 4

250g/9oz/generous 1 cup ricotta cheese

2 egg whites, beaten

60ml/4 tbsp scented honey, plus extra to taste

450g/1lb/4 cups mixed fresh or frozen fruit, such as strawberries, raspberries, blackberries and cherries

1 Preheat the oven to 180°C/350°F/Gas 4. Place the ricotta cheese in a bowl and break it up with a wooden spoon. Add the beaten egg whites and honey, and mix thoroughly until smooth and well combined.

2 Lightly grease four ramekins. Spoon the ricotta mixture into the prepared ramekins and level the tops. Bake for 20 minutes, or until the ricotta cakes are risen and golden.

3 Meanwhile, make the fruit sauce. Reserve about one-quarter of the fruit for decoration. Place the rest of the fruit in a pan, with a little water if the fruit is fresh, and heat gently until softened. Leave to cool slightly and remove any pits if using cherries.

4 Press the fruit through a sieve (strainer), then taste and sweeten with honey if it is too tart. Serve the sauce, warm or cold, with the ricotta cakes. Decorate with the reserved berries.

Variation
You could other soft cheeses for this recipe. Mascarpone would be a good choice, but you could use any fresh, creamy, slightly sweet soft cheese.

Summer Berries: Energy 219kcal/919kJ; Protein 3.9g; Carbohydrate 29.7g, of which sugars 29.7g; Fat 5.6g, of which saturates 1.6g; Cholesterol 202mg; Calcium 50mg; Fibre 1.2g; Sodium 20mg.
Baked Ricotta Cakes: Energy 161kcal/674kJ; Protein 8.1g; Carbohydrate 11.5g, of which sugars 11.5g; Fat 9.6g, of which saturates 5.9g; Cholesterol 26mg; Calcium 23mg; Fibre 0.6g; Sodium 63mg.

Deep-fried Cherries

Fresh fruit coated with a simple batter and then deep-fried is delicious and makes an unusual dessert. These succulent cherries are perfect sprinkled with sugar and cinnamon and served with a classic vanilla ice cream.

Serves 4–6
450g/1lb ripe red cherries, on their stalks
225g/8oz batter mix
1 egg

From the storecupboard
vegetable oil, for deep-frying

1 Gently wash the cherries and pat dry with kitchen paper. Tie the stalks together with fine string to form clusters of four or five cherries.

2 Make up the batter mix according to the instructions on the packet, beating in the egg. Pour the vegetable oil into a deep-fat fryer or large, heavy pan and heat to 190°C/375°F.

3 Working in batches, half-dip each cherry cluster into the batter and then carefully drop the cluster into the hot oil. Fry for 3–4 minutes, or until golden. Remove the deep-fried cherries with a wire-mesh skimmer or slotted spoon and drain on a wire rack placed over crumpled kitchen paper, and serve immediately.

Cook's Tip
To check that the oil has come to the required temperature, drop a cube of day-old bread in the oil, if it turns golden brown and crispy in 20 seconds, the oil is hot enough.

Variation
Other fruits can be deep-fried in batter with delicious results. Bananas work well, especially with a little coconut milk in the batter mix. Ready-to-eat stoned (pitted) prunes, dates or figs can also be used in this recipe

Hot Blackberry and Apple Soufflé

The deliciously tart flavours of blackberry and apple complement each other perfectly to make a light, mouthwatering and surprisingly low-fat, hot dessert. Running a table knife around the inside edge of the soufflé dishes before baking helps the soufflés to rise evenly without sticking to the rim of the dish. Make this dish in early autumn, when there are plentiful supplies of blackberries.

Makes 6
350g/12oz/3 cups blackberries
1 large cooking apple, peeled and finely diced
3 egg whites
150g/5oz/¾ cup caster (superfine) sugar, plus extra caster or icing (confectioners') sugar for dusting

1 Preheat the oven to 200°C/400°F/Gas 6. Put a baking sheet in the oven to heat. Cook the blackberries and apple in a pan for 10 minutes, or until the juice runs from the blackberries and the apple has pulped down well. Press through a sieve (strainer) into a bowl. Stir in 50g/2oz/¼ cup caster sugar. Set aside to cool.

2 Put a spoonful of the fruit purée into each of six 150ml/¼ pint/⅔ cup greased and sugared individual soufflé dishes and smooth the surface. Set the dishes aside.

3 Whisk the egg whites in a large bowl until they form stiff peaks. Gradually whisk in the remaining caster sugar. Fold in the remaining fruit purée and spoon the flavoured meringue into the prepared dishes. Level the tops with a metal spatula and run a table knife around the edge of each dish.

4 Place the dishes on the hot baking sheet and bake for 10–15 minutes, until the soufflés have risen well and are lightly browned. Dust the tops with sugar and serve immediately.

Cook's Tip
If you collect blackberries from the hedgerows, wash thoroughly.

Deep-fried Cherries: Energy 201kcal/840kJ; Protein 3.7g; Carbohydrate 25.7g, of which sugars 7.3g; Fat 10g, of which saturates 1.3g; Cholesterol 26mg; Calcium 46mg; Fibre 1.3g; Sodium 11mg.
Blackberry/Apple Soufflé: Energy 123kcal/522kJ; Protein 2.1g; Carbohydrate 30.1g, of which sugars 30.1g; Fat 0.1g, of which saturates 0g; Cholesterol 0mg; Calcium 38mg; Fibre 2g; Sodium 33mg.

Pumpkin Poached in Syrup

In winter, Turkish markets and streets are alive with busy pumpkin stalls selling pumpkin flesh, prepared especially for this exquisite dish. Serve on its own or with chilled clotted cream or crème fraîche.

Serves 4–6

450g/1lb sugar
juice of 1 lemon
6 cloves
1kg/2¼ lb peeled and deseeded pumpkin flesh, cut into cubes or rectangular blocks

1 Put the sugar into a deep, wide, heavy pan and pour in 250ml/8fl oz/1 cup water. Bring to the boil, stirring continuously, until the sugar has dissolved, then boil gently for 2–3 minutes.

2 Lower the heat and stir in the lemon juice and cloves, then slip in the pumpkin pieces and bring the liquid back to the boil. Lower the heat and put the lid on the pan.

3 Poach the pumpkin gently, turning the pieces over from time to time, until they are tender and a rich, gleaming orange colour. This may take 1½–2 hours, depending on the size of the pumpkin pieces.

4 Leave the pumpkin to cool in the pan, then lift the pieces out of the syrup and place them in a serving dish.

5 Spoon most, or all, of the syrup over the pumpkin pieces and serve at room temperature or chilled.

Variation
This dessert can be varied infinitely by changing the fruit and the syrup flavouring. Another classic Turkish combination uses dried apricots, soaked in water overnight, and lemon juice and orange blossom water to scent the syrup. In this recipe the poached and cooled fruits are filled with Kaymak, a cream made from water buffalo milk, but you could use crème fraîche or clotted cream instead.

Tropical Scented Fruit Salad

With its special colour and exotic flavour, this fresh fruit salad is perfect after a rich, heavy meal. For fabulous flavour and colour, try using three small blood oranges and three ordinary oranges. Other fruit that can be added include pears, kiwi fruit and bananas. Serve this tropical fruit salad with whipping cream flavoured with 15g/½oz finely chopped drained preserved stem ginger.

Serves 4–6

350–400g/12–14oz/3–3½ cups strawberries, hulled and halved
6 oranges, peeled and segmented
1–2 passion fruit
120ml/4fl oz/½ cup medium dry or sweet white wine

1 Put the hulled and halved strawberries and peeled and segmented oranges into a serving bowl. Halve the passion fruit and, using a teaspoon, scoop the flesh into the bowl.

2 Pour the wine over the fruit and toss gently. Cover and chill in the refrigerator until ready to serve.

Cook's Tip
To prepare the oranges, place on a chopping board and slice off the top and bottom to expose the flesh. Stand upright and, using a small sharp knife, slice down between the skin and the flesh. Do this all the way around to remove all the peel and pith. Repeat with the remaining oranges, reserving any juice. Holding one orange over a bowl to catch the juices, cut between the membrane to release the segments. Repeat. Pour any reserved juice over the fruit salad.

Variation
Combine any sweet and tart fruits with contrasting colours.

Pumpkin in Syrup: Energy 317kcal/1353kJ; Protein 1.6g; Carbohydrate 82.1g, of which sugars 81.2g; Fat 0.3g, of which saturates 0.2g; Cholesterol 0mg; Calcium 88mg; Fibre 1.7g; Sodium 5mg.
Tropical Scented Fruit: Energy 81kcal/342kJ; Protein 2g; Carbohydrate 15.6g, of which sugars 15.6g; Fat 0.2g, of which saturates 0g; Cholesterol 0mg; Calcium 75mg; Fibre 3g; Sodium 13mg.

Fresh Fig Compôte with Vanilla and Coffee

A vanilla and coffee syrup brings out the wonderful flavour of figs in this compôte. Serve Greek yogurt or vanilla ice cream with the poached fruit. A wide selection of different honey is available – its aroma and flavour will be subtly scented by the plants surrounding the hives. Orange blossom honey works particularly well in this recipe, although any clear variety is suitable.

Serves 4–6

400ml/14fl oz/1⅔ cups fresh brewed coffee
115g/4oz/½ cup clear honey
1 vanilla pod (bean)
12 slightly underripe fresh figs

1 Choose a frying pan with a lid, large enough to hold the figs in a single layer. Pour in the coffee and add the honey.

2 Split the vanilla pod lengthways and scrape the seeds into the pan. Add the vanilla pod, then bring to a rapid boil and cook until the liquid has reduced to about 175ml/6fl oz/¾ cup.

3 Wash the figs and pierce the skins several times with a sharp skewer. Cut in half and add to the syrup. Reduce the heat, cover and simmer for 5 minutes. Remove the figs from the syrup with a slotted spoon and set aside to cool.

4 Strain the syrup over the figs. Allow to stand at room temperature for 1 hour before serving with Greek (US strained plain) yogurt or vanilla ice cream.

> **Cook's Tip**
> *Figs come in three main varieties – red, white and black – and all three are suitable for cooking. They are sweet and succulent, and complement the stronger, more pervasive flavours of coffee and vanilla very well.*

Oranges in Coffee Syrup

This recipe works well with most citrus fruits – for example, try pink grapefruit or sweet, perfumed clementines, which have been peeled but left whole. Serve the oranges with 300ml/½ pint/1¼ cups whipped cream flavoured with 5ml/1 tsp ground cinnamon or 5ml/1 tsp ground nutmeg, or simply with a spoonful of Greek yogurt.

Serves 6

6 medium oranges
200g/7oz/1 cup sugar
100ml/3½ fl oz/scant ½ cup fresh strong brewed coffee
50g/2oz/½ cup pistachio nuts, chopped (optional)

1 Finely pare, shred and reserve the rind from one orange. Peel the remaining oranges. Cut each one crossways into slices, then re-form them, with a cocktail stick (toothpick) through the centre.

2 Put the sugar in a heavy pan and add 50ml/2fl oz/¼ cup water. Heat gently until the sugar dissolves, then bring to the boil and cook until the syrup turns pale gold.

3 Remove from the heat and carefully pour 100ml/3½fl oz/ scant ½ cup freshly boiling water into the pan. Return to the heat until the syrup has dissolved in the water. Stir in the coffee.

4 Add the oranges and the rind to the coffee syrup. Simmer for 15–20 minutes, turning the oranges once during cooking. Leave to cool, then chill. Serve the oranges and syrup in individual bowls and sprinkle with pistachio nuts, if using.

> **Cook's Tip**
> *Choose a pan in which the oranges will just fit in a single layer – use a deep frying pan if you don't have a pan that is large enough.*

Fresh Fig Compôte: Energy 147kcal/628kJ; Protein 1.7g; Carbohydrate 36g, of which sugars 35.8g; Fat 0.6g, of which saturates 0g; Cholesterol 0mg; Calcium 103mg; Fibre 3g; Sodium 27mg.
Oranges in Syrup: Energy 191kcal/815kJ; Protein 2g; Carbohydrate 48.5g, of which sugars 48.5g; Fat 0.2g, of which saturates 0g; Cholesterol 0mg; Calcium 93mg; Fibre 2.7g; Sodium 10mg.

Juniper-scented Pears in Red Wine

More often used in savoury dishes than sweet, juniper berries have a dark blue, almost black colour with a distinct gin-like flavour. In this fruity winter dessert crushed juniper berries give the classic partnership of pears and red wine a slightly aromatic flavour. These pears are particularly good sprinkled with toasted almonds and whipped cream.

Serves 4
30ml/2 tbsp juniper berries
50g/2oz/¼ cup caster (superfine) sugar
600ml/1 pint/2½ cups red wine
4 large or 8 small firm pears, stalks intact

1 Lightly crush the juniper berries using a pestle and mortar or with the end of a rolling pin. Put the berries in a pan with the sugar and wine and heat gently until the sugar dissolves.

2 Meanwhile, peel the pears carefully, leaving them whole and with the stalks left on. Add them to the wine and heat until just simmering. Cover the pan and cook gently for about 25 minutes, until the pears are tender. Turn the pears once or twice to make sure they cook evenly.

3 Use a slotted spoon to remove the pears. Boil the syrup hard for a few minutes, until it is slightly reduced and thickened. If serving the pears hot, reheat them gently in the syrup, otherwise arrange them in a serving dish and spoon the syrup over.

Variations
• Use ruby port or Madeira wine instead of red wine for a sweeter, more intense flavour.
• Substitute other fruits depending on the season. For example, in late summer you could use ripe plums, apples or blackberries.

Pistachio and Rose Water Oranges

This light and citrusy dessert is perfect to serve after a heavy main course, such as a hearty meat stew or a leg of roast lamb. Combining three favourite Middle Eastern ingredients, it is delightfully fragrant and refreshing. If you don't have pistachio nuts, use hazelnuts instead.

Serves 4
4 large oranges
30ml/2 tbsp rose water
30ml/2 tbsp shelled pistachio nuts, roughly chopped

1 Slice the top and bottom off one of the oranges to expose the flesh. Using a small serrated knife, slice down between the pith and the flesh, working round the orange, to remove all the peel and pith. Slice the orange into six rounds, reserving any juice. Repeat with the remaining oranges.

2 Arrange the orange rounds on a serving dish. Mix the reserved juice with the rose water and drizzle the liquid over the oranges.

3 Cover the dish with clear film (plastic wrap) and chill for about 30 minutes. Sprinkle the chopped pistachio nuts over the oranges to serve.

Cook's Tip
Rose-scented sugar is delicious sprinkled over fresh fruit salads. Wash and thoroughly dry a handful of rose petals and place in a sealed container filled with caster (superfine) sugar for 2–3 days. Remove the petals before using the sugar.

Variation
Almonds could be used instead of pistachio nuts for this dish and orange blossom water could replace rose water.

Pistachio Oranges: Energy 101kcal/424kJ; Protein 3g; Carbohydrate 13.4g, of which sugars 13.2g; Fat 4.3g, of which saturates 0.6g; Cholesterol 0mg; Calcium 79mg; Fibre 3g; Sodium 47mg.
Juniper-scented Pears: Energy 378kcal/1595kJ; Protein 1g; Carbohydrate 65.7g, of which sugars 65.7g; Fat 0.2g, of which saturates 0g; Cholesterol 0mg; Calcium 53mg; Fibre 3.9g; Sodium 22mg.

Gooseberry Fool

This quickly made dessert never fails to impress. Blackberries, raspberries, blackcurrants or rhubarb work well in place of gooseberries. When using young pink rhubarb there is no need to sieve the cooked fruit. Serve in pretty glasses with small crisp biscuits to provide a contrast in texture.

Serves 4
450g/1lb chopped gooseberries
125g/4½oz/¼ cup caster
   (superfine) sugar, or to taste
300ml/½ pint/1¼ cups double
   (heavy) cream

1 Put the gooseberries into a pan with 30ml/2 tbsp water. Cover and cook gently for about 10 minutes, until the fruit is soft. Stir in the sugar to taste.

2 Transfer the fruit into a nylon sieve (strainer) and press through. Leave the purée to cool.

3 Whip the cream until stiff enough to hold soft peaks. Stir in the gooseberry purée without over-mixing (it looks pretty with some streaks).

4 Spoon the mixture into serving glasses and refrigerate until you are ready to eat.

Mango and Lime Fool

Canned mangoes are used here for convenience, but this zesty, tropical fruit fool tastes even better if made with the superior fresh ones. Choose a variety with a good flavour, such as the fragrant Alphonso mango.

Serves 4
400g/14oz can sliced mango, plus
   extra to garnish (optional)
grated rind of 1 lime, plus juice
   of ½ lime
150ml/¼ pint/⅔ cup double
   (heavy) cream
90ml/6 tbsp Greek (US strained
   plain) yogurt

1 Drain the canned mango slices and put them in a food processor, then add the grated lime rind and lime juice. Process until the mixture forms a smooth purée.

2 Alternatively, place the mango slices in a bowl and mash with a potato masher, then press through a sieve (strainer) into a bowl with the back of a wooden spoon. Stir in the lime rind and juice.

3 Pour the cream into a bowl and add the yogurt. Whisk until the mixture is thick and then quickly whisk in the mango mixture.

4 Spoon the fool into four tall cups or glasses and chill for at least 1 hour. Just before serving, decorate each glass with fresh mango slices, if you like. Serve with small crunchy biscuits (cookies) for a contrasting texture.

Rhubarb and Ginger Jellies

Made with bright pink, young rhubarb, these softly set jellies get the taste buds tingling. They are spiced with plenty of fresh ginger, which gives just a hint of zesty warmth. Pour the jelly into pretty glasses and serve it as it is or top it with spoonfuls of lightly whipped cream.

Serves 5–6
1kg/2¼lb young rhubarb
200g/7oz/1 cup caster
   (superfine) sugar
50g/2oz fresh root ginger,
   finely chopped
15ml/1 tbsp powdered
   vegetarian gelatine

1 Cut the rhubarb into 2cm/¾in chunks and place in a pan with the sugar and ginger.

2 Pour in 450ml/¾ pint/scant 2 cups water and bring to the boil. Reduce the heat, cover and simmer gently for 10 minutes, until the rhubarb is very soft and pulpy.

3 Meanwhile, sprinkle the gelatine over 30ml/2 tbsp cold water in a small heatproof bowl. Leave to stand, without stirring, for 5 minutes, until the gelatine has become sponge-like in texture.

4 Set the bowl over a small pan of hot water and simmer, stirring occasionally, until the gelatine has dissolved completely into a clear liquid. Remove from the heat.

5 Strain the cooked rhubarb through a fine sieve (strainer) into a bowl. Stir in the dissolved gelatine until thoroughly mixed. Leave to cool slightly before pouring into serving glasses. Chill for at least 4 hours or overnight, until set.

> **Variation**
> *There are endless possibilities on the theme of fruit jellies. A classic English combination is raspberry and white wine, but you could equally use clementines and grape juice or just about any other combination. You can make your life really easy by simply using a carton of juice and vegetarian gelatine.*

Gooseberry Fool: Energy 517kcal/2147kJ; Protein 2.6g; Carbohydrate 37.3g, of which sugars 37.3g; Fat 40.7g, of which saturates 25.1g; Cholesterol 103mg; Calcium 85mg; Fibre 2.7g; Sodium 21mg.
Mango Fool: Energy 269kcal/1118kJ; Protein 2.8g; Carbohydrate 15.2g, of which sugars 14.9g; Fat 22.6g, of which saturates 13.8g; Cholesterol 51mg; Calcium 64mg; Fibre 2.6g; Sodium 26mg.
Rhubarb Jellies: Energy 152kcal/652kJ; Protein 3.8g; Carbohydrate 36.2g, of which sugars 36.2g; Fat 0.2g, of which saturates 0g; Cholesterol 0mg; Calcium 176mg; Fibre 2.4g; Sodium 12mg.

Rhubarb and Ginger Trifles

Choose a good quality jar of rhubarb compôte for this recipe; try to find one with large, chunky pieces of fruit. Alternatively, make your own by poaching in sugar and water.

Serves 4
12 gingernut biscuits (gingersnaps)
50ml/2fl oz/¼ cup rhubarb compôte
450ml/¾ pint/scant 2 cups extra thick double (heavy) cream

1 Put the ginger biscuits in a plastic bag and seal. Bash the biscuits with a rolling pin until roughly crushed.

2 Set aside two tablespoons of crushed biscuits and divide the rest among four glasses.

3 Spoon the rhubarb compôte on top of the crushed biscuits, then top with the cream. Place in the refrigerator and chill for about 30 minutes.

4 To serve, sprinkle the reserved crushed biscuits over the trifles and serve immediately.

Cook's Tip
To make a rhubarb compôte, take 450g/1lb rhubarb, trimmed, cut into pieces and wash thoroughly. Put in a pan with 75g/3oz/½ cup soft light brown sugar (and a little ginger wine if desired) and place over a low heat for about 10 minutes.

Variation
You can make many versions of this dessert by varying the fruit, the type of biscuit (cookie) and the topping. Stewed plums or peaches would make a good choice. Alternatively, use a summer fruits or apricot compôte. Any type of crunchy biscuit can be used, but amaretti would be excellent. In place of the extra thick double (heavy) cream use Greek (US strained plain) yogurt or crème fraîche.

Crispy Mango Stacks with Raspberry Coulis

This makes a very healthy yet stunning dessert – it is low in fat and contains no added sugar. However, if the raspberries are a little sharp, you may prefer to add a pinch of sugar to the purée.

Serves 4
3 filo pastry sheets, thawed if frozen
2 small ripe mangoes
115g/4oz/⅔ raspberries, thawed if frozen

From the storecupboard
50g/2oz/¼ cup butter, melted

1 Preheat the oven to 200°C/400°F/Gas 6. Lay the filo sheets on a clean work surface and cut out four 10cm/4in rounds from each.

2 Brush each round with the melted butter and lay the rounds on two baking sheets. Bake for 5 minutes, or until crisp and golden. Place on wire racks to cool.

3 Peel the mangoes, remove the stones (pits) and cut the flesh into thin slices.

4 Put the raspberries in a food processor with 45ml/3 tbsp water and process to a purée. Place a pastry round on each of four serving plates.

5 Top with a quarter of the mango and drizzle with a little of the raspberry purée. Repeat until all the ingredients have been used, finishing with a layer of mango and a drizzle of raspberry purée.

Variation
This dessert could be made with many fruit combinations. The main things to consider are the complementary colours and the contrast of sweetness and sharpness in the fruit. Peach and strawberry is just one example.

Rhubarb Trifles: Energy 695kcal/2874kJ; Protein 3.6g; Carbohydrate 27.1g, of which sugars 14.1g; Fat 64.3g, of which saturates 39.4g; Cholesterol 154mg; Calcium 98mg; Fibre 0.6g; Sodium 124mg.
Mango Stacks: Energy 186kcal/779kJ; Protein 2.2g; Carbohydrate 21.7g, of which sugars 11.9g; Fat 10.7g, of which saturates 6.7g; Cholesterol 27mg; Calcium 36mg; Fibre 3.1g; Sodium 79mg.

Tangy Raspberry and Lemon Tartlets

Fresh raspberries teamed with a sharp lemon curd create colourful and tangy tartlets. Choose a top quality lemon curd for the best result.

Serves 4

175g/6oz ready-made short-crust pastry, thawed if frozen
120ml/8 tbsp good quality lemon curd
115g/4oz/⅔ cup fresh raspberries

1 Preheat the oven to 190°C/375°F/Gas 5. Roll out the pastry and use to line four 9cm/3½in tartlet tins (muffin pans). Line each tin with a circle of baking parchment and fill with baking beans or uncooked rice.

2 Bake for 15–20 minutes, or until golden and cooked through. Remove the baking beans or rice and paper and take the pastry cases out of the tins. Leave them to cool completely on a wire rack.

3 Set aside 12 raspberries for decoration and fold the remaining ones into the lemon curd. Spoon the mixture into the pastry cases and top with the reserved raspberries. Serve immediately.

Cook's Tips
• *To save on last-minute preparation time, you can make the pastry cases (pie shells) for these little tartlets in advance and store them in an airtight container until ready to serve.*
• *For an attractive finish, dust the tartlets with sifted icing (confectioners') sugar and decorate with mint sprigs.*

Variation
Stir a little whipped cream or crème fraîche into the lemon curd for a creamy, luxurious finish, or serve with whipped cream on the side.

Strawberry Cream Shortbreads

Simple to assemble, these pretty strawberry desserts are always popular. Serve them as soon as they are ready, because the shortbread biscuits will lose their lovely crisp texture if left to stand.

Serves 3

150g/5oz/ generous 1 cup strawberries
450ml/¾ pint/scant 2 cups double (heavy) cream
6 round shortbread biscuits (cookies)
fresh mint sprigs, to decorate (optional)

1 Reserve three strawberries for decoration. Hull the remaining strawberries and cut them in half.

2 Put the halved strawberries in a bowl and gently crush using the back of a fork. (Only crush the berries lightly; they should not be reduced to a purée.)

3 Put the cream in a large, clean bowl and whip to form soft peaks. Add the crushed strawberries and gently fold in to combine. (Do not overmix.)

4 Halve the reserved strawberries, then spoon the strawberry and cream mixture on top of the shortbread biscuits. Decorate each one with half a strawberry and serve immediately.

Cook's Tip
To decorate, you can use whole strawberries and give them a pretty frosted effect by painting them with egg white and dipping in caster (superfine) sugar. Leave them to dry before using and add a mint sprig.

Variation
You can use any other berry you like for this dessert – try raspberries or blueberries. Two ripe, peeled peaches will also give great results.

Raspberry Tartlets: Energy 289kcal/1214kJ; Protein 3.1g; Carbohydrate 40.6g, of which sugars 13.8g; Fat 13.9g, of which saturates 4.3g; Cholesterol 13mg; Calcium 47mg; Fibre 1.6g; Sodium 195mg.
Shortbreads: Energy 976kcal/4035kJ; Protein 5.7g; Carbohydrate 34.6g, of which sugars 16.8g; Fat 90.8g, of which saturates 50.1g; Cholesterol 206mg; Calcium 122mg; Fibre 1.3g; Sodium 204mg.

Tomato and Cucumber Juice with Basil

Basil is an excellent herb for juicing, keeping its distinctive fresh fragrance. It makes the perfect partner for mild, refreshing cucumber and the sweetest, juiciest tomatoes you can find – use cherry tomatoes for an extra sweet flavour.

Serves 1–2
½ cucumber, peeled
a handful of fresh basil
350g/12oz tomatoes

1 Quarter the cucumber lengthways. There's no need to remove the seeds. Push it through a juicer with the basil, then do the same with the tomatoes.

2 Pour the tomato, basil and cucumber juice over ice cubes in one tall or two short glasses and echo the herb flavour by adding a few basil sprigs for decoration.

Beetroot, Ginger and Orange Juice

Despite its firmness, beetroot can be juiced raw and its intense flavour goes perfectly with tangy citrus fruits and fresh root ginger.

Serves 1
200g/7oz raw beetroot (beets)
1cm/½in piece fresh root ginger, peeled
1 large orange

1 Scrub the beetroot, then trim them and slice them into quarters. Push half the beetroot through a vegetable juicer, followed by the ginger and the remaining beetroot and pour the juice into a jug (pitcher).

2 Squeeze the juice from the orange, using a citrus juicer or by hand, and pour into the beetroot juice. Stir to combine.

3 Pour the juice over ice cubes in a glass and serve immediately to enjoy the full benefit of all the nutrients. (Do not let the ice cubes melt into the juice or they will dilute its flavour.)

Carrot Revitalizer

This vibrant combination of vegetables and fruit makes a lively, health-giving drink. Carrots yield generous quantities of sweet juice, which goes perfectly with the sharp flavour of pear and the zesty taste of orange. This powerful drink will nourish and stimulate the system.

Serves 1
3 carrots
2 apples
1 orange

1 Scrub and trim the carrots and quarter the apples. Peel the orange and cut into rough segments.

2 Using a juice extractor, juice the carrots and fruit, pour into a glass and serve immediately.

Purple Pep

Jewel-coloured beetroot juice is well known for its detoxifying properties, so this juice makes the perfect choice when you've been over-doing it, offering an excellent supply of valuable essential nutrients.

Serves 1
3 carrots
115g/4oz beetroot (beet)
25g/1oz baby spinach, washed and dried
2 celery sticks

1 Scrub and trim the carrots and beetroot. Using a sharp knife, cut the beetroot into large chunks.

2 Using a juice extractor, juice the carrots, beetroot, spinach and celery, then pour into a glass and serve immediately.

Cook's Tip
Beetroot has the highest sugar content of any vegetable and makes a delicious juice with a rich but refreshing taste.

Tomato Juice: Energy 40kcal/168kJ; Protein 1.9g; Carbohydrate 7g, of which sugars 6.8g; Fat 0.7g, of which saturates 0.2g; Cholesterol 0mg; Calcium 31mg; Fibre 2.4g; Sodium 19mg.
Beetroot Juice: Energy 116kcal/498kJ; Protein 4.7g; Carbohydrate 25.4g, of which sugars 24.2g; Fat 0.3g, of which saturates 0g; Cholesterol 0mg; Calcium 96mg; Fibre 5.8g; Sodium 138mg.
Carrot Revitalizer: Energy 160kcal/678kJ; Protein 2.9g; Carbohydrate 37.6g, of which sugars 36.6g; Fat 0.8g, of which saturates 0.2g; Cholesterol 0mg; Calcium 112mg; Fibre 8.9g; Sodium 59mg.
Purple Pep: Energy 122kcal/513kJ; Protein 4.2g; Carbohydrate 25.5g, of which sugars 23.8g; Fat 1g, of which saturates 0.2g; Cholesterol 0mg; Calcium 140mg; Fibre 8.2g; Sodium 197mg.

Leafy Apple Lift-off

This delicious blend of fruit and fresh green leaves is refreshing and healthy. The leaves are robustly flavoured and have a peppery, pungent taste. To prepare the leaves, discard any damaged and discoloured ones and rinse thoroughly in cold water to remove any grit. To prevent the juice from being watery, dry the leaves in a salad spinner or on kitchen paper before juicing.

Serves I
I eating apple
150g/5oz white grapes
25g/1oz watercress, rocket
  (arugula) or spinach
15ml/1 tbsp lime juice

I Quarter the apple. Using a juice extractor, juice the fruit and watercress, rocket or spinach.

2 Add the lime juice to the apple, grape and leaf mixture and stir thoroughly to blend all the ingredients together. Pour the juice into a tall glass and serve immediately.

Fennel Fusion

The hearty combination of raw vegetables and apples makes a surprisingly delicious juice that is packed with natural goodness and is a truly wonderful pick-me-up for those times when you are depleted of energy.

Serves I
½ small red cabbage
½ fennel bulb
2 eating apples
15ml/1 tbsp lemon juice

I Coarsely slice the red cabbage and the fennel bulb and quarter the eating apples. Using a juice extractor, juice the vegetables and fruit.

2 Add the lemon juice to the red cabbage, fennel and apple mixture and stir thoroughly to blend all the ingredients together. Pour into a glass and serve immediately.

Melon Pick-me-up

Spicy fresh root ginger is delicious with melon and pear in this reviving and invigorating concoction. Charentais or Galia melon can be used instead of the cantaloupe melon. To enjoy fresh root ginger at its best, keep in a cool, dry place for up to a week.

Serves I
½ cantaloupe melon
2 pears
2.5cm/1in piece of fresh
  root ginger

I Quarter the cantaloupe melon, remove the seeds, and carefully slice the flesh away from the skin, reserving any juice. Quarter the pears and reserve any juice.

2 Using a juice extractor, juice the melon flesh and juice, quartered pears and juice and the fresh root ginger. Pour the juice into a tall glass and serve immediately.

Apple Shiner

This refreshing fusion of sweet apple, honeydew melon, red grapes and lemon provides a reviving burst of energy and a feel-good sensation. Serve as a drink or use to pour over muesli for a quick and healthy breakfast.

Serves I
I eating apple
½ honeydew melon
90g/3½ oz red grapes
15ml/1 tbsp lemon juice

I Quarter the apple and remove the core. Cut the melon into quarters, remove the seeds and slice the flesh away from the skin.

2 Using a juice extractor, juice the apple, melon and grapes. Alternatively, process the fruit in a food processor or blender for 2–3 minutes, until smooth. Pour the juice into a long, tall glass, stir in the lemon juice and serve immediately.

Leafy Apple Lift-off: Energy 120kcal/512kJ; Protein 1.5g; Carbohydrate 29.5g, of which sugars 29.4g; Fat 0.4g, of which saturates 0g; Cholesterol 0mg; Calcium 65mg; Fibre 2.6g; Sodium 39mg.
Fennel Fusion: Energy 142kcal/600kJ; Protein 5.5g; Carbohydrate 29.3g, of which sugars 28.9g; Fat 0.9g, of which saturates 0g; Cholesterol 0mg; Calcium 177mg; Fibre 10.9g; Sodium 35mg.
Melon Pick-me-up: Energy 240kcal/1017kJ; Protein 3.4g; Carbohydrate 58g, of which sugars 58g; Fat 0.8g, of which saturates 0g; Cholesterol 0mg; Calcium 98mg; Fibre 8.6g; Sodium 164mg.
Apple Shiner: Energy 197kcal/842kJ; Protein 3.1g; Carbohydrate 47.8g, of which sugars 47.8g; Fat 0.7g, of which saturates 0g; Cholesterol 0mg; Calcium 79mg; Fibre 3.7g; Sodium 158mg.

Citrus Sparkle

Pink grapefruit have a sweeter flavour than the yellow varieties – in fact, the pinker they are, the sweeter they are likely to be.

Serves 1

1 pink grapefruit
1 orange
30ml/2 tbsp freshly squeezed
   lemon juice

1 Cut the pink grapefruit and orange in half and squeeze out the juice using a citrus fruit squeezer. Pour the juice into a glass, stir in 15ml/1 tbsp lemon juice, add the remaining lemon juice if required and serve.

Cranberry and Spice Spritzer

Partially freezing fruit juice gives it a refreshingly slushy texture. The combination of cranberry and apple juice is tart and clean. Add a few fresh or frozen cranberries to decorate each glass, if you like.

Serves 4

600ml/1 pint/2½ cups chilled
   cranberry juice
150ml/¼ pint/⅔ cup clear
   apple juice
4 cinnamon sticks
about 400ml/14fl oz/1⅔ cups
   chilled ginger ale

1 Pour the cranberry juice into a shallow freezerproof container and freeze for about 2 hours, or until a thick layer of ice crystals has formed around the edges. Mash the semi-frozen juice with a fork, then return the mixture to the freezer for 2–3 hours, until almost solid.

2 Pour the apple juice into a small pan, add two cinnamon sticks and bring to just below boiling point. Pour into a jug (pitcher) and leave to cool, then remove the cinnamon sticks and set them aside. Cool, then chill the juice.

3 Spoon the cranberry ice into a food processor or blender. Add the cinnamon-flavoured apple juice and process briefly until slushy. Pile the mixture into cocktail glasses, top up with chilled ginger ale, decorate with cinnamon sticks and serve.

Blue Lagoon

Blackcurrants are not only an excellent source of betacarotene and vitamin C, but they are also rich in flavonoids, which help to cleanse the system. Mixed with other dark red fruits, such as blackberries and grapes, they make a highly nutritious and extremely delicious blend that can be refrigerated and enjoyed throughout the day.

Serves 1

90g/3½ oz/scant 1 cup
   blackcurrants or blackberries
150g/5oz red grapes
130g/4½ oz/generous 1 cup
   blueberries

1 If you are using blackcurrants, gently pull the stalks through the tines of a fork to remove the fruit. Next remove the stalks from the grapes.

2 Push all the fruits through a juicer, saving a few for decoration. Place some ice in a medium glass and pour over the juice. Decorate with the reserved fruit and serve.

Hum-zinger

Aromatic tropical fruits make a drink that is bursting with flavour and energy. Enjoy a glass first thing in the morning to kick-start your day.

Serves 1

½ pineapple, peeled
1 small mango, peeled and
   stoned (pitted)
½ small papaya, seeded
   and peeled

1 Remove any 'eyes' left in the pineapple, then cut all the fruit into fairly coarse chunks.

2 Using a juice extractor, juice the fruit. Alternatively, use a food processor or blender and process for about 2–3 minutes until smooth. Pour into a glass and serve immediately.

Citrus Sparkle: Energy 92kcal/391kJ; Protein 2.6g; Carbohydrate 21.1g, of which sugars 21.1g; Fat 0.3g, of which saturates 0g; Cholesterol 0mg; Calcium 93mg; Fibre 4.1g; Sodium 11mg.
Cranberry and Spice: Energy 86kcal/370kJ; Protein 0.2g; Carbohydrate 22.5g, of which sugars 22.5g; Fat 0.2g, of which saturates 0g; Cholesterol 0mg; Calcium 13mg; Fibre 0g; Sodium 4mg.
Blue Lagoon: Energy 189kcal/805kJ; Protein 2.7g; Carbohydrate 47.2g, of which sugars 42g; Fat 0.2g, of which saturates 0g; Cholesterol 0mg; Calcium 74mg; Fibre 6.9g; Sodium 6mg.
Hum-zinger: Energy 322kcal/1378kJ; Protein 3.7g; Carbohydrate 79.1g, of which sugars 78.7g; Fat 1.3g, of which saturates 0.1g; Cholesterol 0mg; Calcium 136mg; Fibre 13.1g; Sodium 21mg.

New York Egg Cream

No one knows precisely why this legendary drink is called egg cream, but some say it was an ironic way of describing its richness at a time when no one could afford to put both expensive eggs and cream together in a drink.

Serves 1
45–60ml/3–4 tbsp good quality
   chocolate syrup
120ml/4fl oz/½ cup chilled milk
175ml/6fl oz/¾ cup chilled
   sparkling mineral water
unsweetened cocoa powder,
   to decorate

1 Carefully pour the chocolate syrup into the bottom of a tall glass, avoiding dripping any on the inside of the glass.

2 Pour the chilled milk into the glass on to the chocolate syrup.

3 Gradually pour the chilled sparkling mineral water into the glass, sip up any foam that rises to the top of the glass and carefully continue to add the remaining chilled sparkling mineral water. Stir well and sprinkle with cocoa powder before drinking.

Chocolate Brownie Milkshake

This truly indulgent drink is so simple, yet utterly luxurious, so take a quiet moment to sit back, relax and enjoy. For an even more indulgent treat, add whipped cream and sprinkle with grated chocolate to serve.

Serves 1
40g/1½ oz chocolate brownies
200ml/7fl oz/scant 1 cup full
   cream (whole) milk
2 scoops vanilla ice cream

1 Crumble the chocolate brownies into a food processor or blender and add the milk. Blend until the mixture is smooth.

2 Add the ice cream to the chocolate milk mixture and blend until the shake is really smooth and frothy. Pour into a tall glass and serve immediately.

Banana and Maple Flip

This satisfying drink is packed with so much goodness that it makes a complete breakfast in a glass – great for when you're in a hurry. Be sure to use a really fresh, free-range egg. The glass can be decorated with a slice of orange or lime to serve.

Serves 1
1 small banana, peeled
   and halved
50ml/2fl oz/¼ cup thick Greek
   (US strained plain) yogurt
1 egg
30ml/2 tbsp maple syrup

1 Put the peeled and halved banana, thick Greek yogurt, egg and maple syrup in a food processor or blender. Add 30ml/ 2 tbsp chilled water.

2 Process the ingredients constantly for about 2 minutes, or until the mixture turns a really pale, creamy colour and has a nice frothy texture.

3 Pour the banana and maple flip into a tall, chilled glass and serve immediately. Decorate the glass with an orange or lime slice, if you like.

Cook's Tips
• To chill the drinking glass quickly, place it in the freezer while you are preparing the drink.
• If you don't have a heavy-duty food processor or blender, crush the ice before adding it.

Variations
• For a more exotic tropical fruit flavour, substitute a small, very ripe, peeled and stoned mango for the banana.
• For a hint of sharpness, add 5ml/1 tsp lemon or lime juice or use a slightly tangy yogurt.
• Use a fat-free natural (plain) yogurt for a low-fat version.

New York Cream: Energy 302kcal/1266kJ; Protein 6.9g; Carbohydrate 32.9g, of which sugars 32.5g; Fat 16.9g, of which saturates 5.8g; Cholesterol 8mg; Calcium 202mg; Fibre 0.4g; Sodium 74mg.
Chocolate Milkshake: Energy 637kcal/2652kJ; Protein 15.4g; Carbohydrate 54.4g, of which sugars 45.5g; Fat 41g, of which saturates 18.6g; Cholesterol 28mg; Calcium 416mg; Fibre 0g; Sodium 348mg.
Banana and Maple Flip: Energy 296kcal/1248kJ; Protein 10.5g; Carbohydrate 43.3g, of which sugars 41.4g; Fat 10.9g, of which saturates 4.2g; Cholesterol 190mg; Calcium 113mg; Fibre 0.9g; Sodium 187mg.

Index

31901051155655